The Charming

PREDATOR

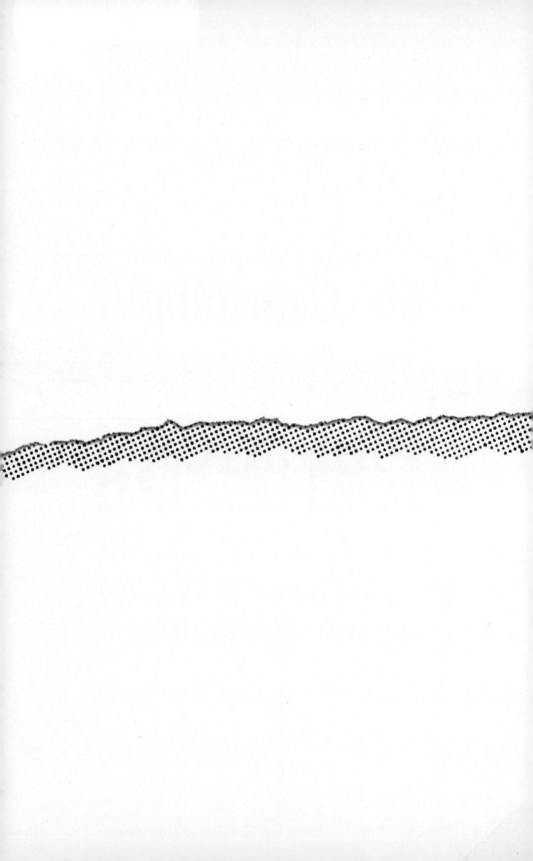

Lee Mackenzie

The Charming

PREDATOR

The True Story of How I Fell in Love with
and Married a Sociopathic Fraud

Doubleday Canada

Doubleday Canada and colophon are registered trademarks of Penguin Random
House Canada Limited

Library and Archives Canada Cataloguing in Publication

Mackenzie, Lee (Donna Lee), author
    The charming predator / Lee Mackenzie.

Issued in print and electronic formats.
ISBN 978-0-385-68712-6 (paperback).—ISBN 978-0-385-68713-3 (epub)

1. Jones, Kenner. 2. Mackenzie, Lee (Donna Lee). 3. Impostors
and imposture—Wales—Biography. 4. Swindlers and swindling—Wales—
Biography. I. Title.

HV6761.W32M33 2017   364.16'3092   C2016-903848-3
                                                  C2016-903849-1

Library of Congress Control Number is available upon request

Cover and text design: Andrew Roberts
Front cover photo courtesy of the author

Printed and bound in the USA

Doubleday Canada
a division of Penguin Random House Canada Limited

www.penguinrandomhouse.ca

1   2   3   4   5   21   20   19   18   17

 Penguin
Random House
DOUBLEDAY CANADA

Dedicated to my mother, Donna,
and to the memory of Kenner's mother, Primrose.

CONTENTS

PROLOGUE

U ntil you've been duped by someone like Kenner
Jones you think it could never happen to you. That's
what I thought, too.

This is the true story of how I met, fell in love with
and married a man who, unbeknownst to me, was an
imposter—a con man of great skill and outrageous audacity. As I eventually learned, he had been in and out of
courts and prisons in Britain before I encountered him.
His deceptions and criminal activities continued for
decades after we split up.

Ask anyone who's met him and you will hear the same
thing: Kenner is one of the most intelligent, charming,
entertaining people they have ever come across. He is easy
to like and easy to believe. I liked him. I believed him.
Although there were clues, I did not clearly see his dark
side until it was too late. He shattered me emotionally,
psychologically and financially.

When I first met Kenner in 1979 while travelling in

Wales, I was a strange combination of capable and inexperienced. On the one hand, I was studying broadcast journalism and honing my skills of observation and objectivity. On the other hand, I was unworldly and naive, the product of a small, rural, western Canadian community.

In my childhood home, what have since become nostalgic clichés were then just facts of life. It was a different time, a time when life was simple and direct. We never locked our doors. If we needed to borrow a cup of sugar and our neighbour wasn't home, we'd just go in, get the sugar, leave a note on the table—and later return the sugar the same way. As children, we scampered through our community carefree and trusting. I can't remember anyone who faced each day saddled with a hefty load of skepticism.

This is not to say I had a perfect childhood. There were family problems, as there often are. The ones in mine left me with some deep emotional scarring that I only came to understand decades later. The young woman travelling through Wales was searching for her roots, soaking up the culture and beauty of the place. Somewhere in the back of my mind I was also wondering if Wales was where I could make a new start, dream my dreams and have them come true.

Initially I didn't envisage Kenner as part of my life—in fact, he didn't appeal to me on first acquaintance. But as he wove his web around me, I heard everything I wanted to hear, saw everything I wanted to see, believed all my dreams were possible. The journalist side of me, which could have helped me with better perception and reason, was not allowed to present its case. I know it wanted me to make an unbiased assessment of the information before me. But there was a lot at stake if I did. If I was wrong about Kenner and our life together, I would have to admit to poor judgment, and I would be picking up a hammer and shattering my own dreams. So I didn't look. I didn't challenge. I didn't take myself away to safety. I just hoped and prayed that it was all going to work out.

The first chapters of this book are based in part on the family history Kenner's mother, Primrose, related to me when I first met her in the summer of 1979. I was just a traveller passing through her town, likely never to be seen again. I realize now I was the perfect listener for her. She could bare her soul, imagining I would forget everything as soon as I left Wales.

I've always had an excellent memory and can easily recall details. When I think of her telling me about her life, I can still hear her voice.

Although I have invented much of Primrose's direct speech, the details of personalities and places are true to her telling, as are her emotions as she described them. Her personality, in equal measures feisty and soft, was still shining through when I knew her.

The stories of Kenner's early years come from events as Primrose told them to me. Again, I invent conversations and some details, but the bones of the stories are true. It wasn't difficult to place Kenner as a child in a home rife with rules and friction.

Kenner's *Doomsday Book* was once in my possession, but I now have only photocopies of a few pages. I loaned the book to someone who was going to do a psychological analysis of it—but who never returned it. If you're reading this now, I'd like it back.

My name may need some clarification. In my childhood, my family called me Donna Lee. As a teenager, I was simply Donna. When I went into broadcasting, I started going by Lee, and still do. I answer to them all! When Kenner and I met, I was Donna, but he never used that name—he always called me Don. His father was John Elias Jones. His mother, when she married John, became Primrose Elias Jones. For a brief time, I duly became Donna Lee Elias Jones.

Kenner's names are even more numerous than mine. Although I called him Kenner, most people simply used Ken. In what can only be a continuing effort to slip through the world without leaving traces, his name has appeared in many variations and inventions. So in addition to Kenner Elias Jones, he has styled himself Elias Jones, Ken Jones, Kenner Jones, Ken Elias Jones, Kenwyn Jones, Kenner Merddyn (Welsh for Merlin) Jones, Kenner Hawkins (Hawkins was Primrose's maiden name), Kenner Hager (the surname of his second wife), Kenner Hawkins Hager, Kenner Ngeiwo (a name he apparently gave himself in Kenya) and Kenner or even Kenneth Ngeiwo Hawkins. I am under no illusions that this is a complete list. Also, he has found many creative ways to present himself, posing variously and entirely falsely as a medical doctor, a deacon, a priest and a philanthropist.

I stashed the pictures, papers and memories from my short, confusing, dramatic time with Kenner in a cardboard box in the storage room and left them all in the dark for decades. The sheer embarrassment of being hoodwinked so easily and completely was too painful to admit to myself, let alone the rest of the world. But time has slowly and effectively done its work. Experience, and the learning that comes with it, has helped me understand myself and, more important, show a measure of compassion and forgiveness for the young woman who stumbled and fell.

In the years following my time with Kenner I had to find a delicate balance: how to live with reality, whatever it might be, yet not lose the ability to love, trust and hope. I also had to find my own way to peace. Even so, I admit I was not only curious but also nervous when I finally opened that old cardboard box for one more look at what was inside.

CHAPTER 1

A Solitary Traveller

Conwy Castle, tucked into a corner of North Wales, was the first real castle I had ever seen. As I gazed at it, I let the weight of my backpack slide off my shoulders and drop to the ground. I was twenty-six years old and had travelled from my home in British Columbia on the west coast of Canada. Conwy, with its rustic, rounded storybook towers and turrets, was a sight right out of my childhood imaginings.

The bus had stopped at Llandudno Junction across the bridge from Conwy. The road sign pointed to the village of Deganwy and the town of Llandudno in one direction, Colwyn Bay in the other and Conwy straight ahead. How to decide?

On impulse I turned toward Llandudno.

I walked right through the main part of the town, drawn by the open space and the sounds of the ocean.

Llandudno's graceful crescent beach was soon before me, winding gently from the Great Orme to the Little Orme at the far end of the waterfront. *Orme* is the Welsh word for "headland." The Great Orme is a huge, stratified mound of granite that was a favourite haunt of the Druids. Many a windswept ceremonial group has trudged and chanted on the shoulders of the Great Orme.

Tall, pastel-coloured hotels crowded side by side, facing the stormy sea. In front of the hotels a wide, paved promenade followed the curve of the bay.

I stood there, soaking up the sight and smell of the sea, then looked right and left on the promenade. I could see a green hut bearing the sign of the Welsh Tourist Board. I headed over.

There was barely enough room for my pack and me both to get through the doorway. Two travellers were already there, making inquiries. When they left, I went up to the counter.

"Hello!" said the tourist officer. "Can I be of assistance?"

He had a pleasant voice and spoke with the musically urgent accent of the North Welsh. He was short—only about five feet five inches tall—and had dark hair that wound itself into large curls, softening his face and warming his blue-grey eyes. He had a scruffy three-week-old beard. He smiled warmly, and made me feel as though I had his full attention and plenty of time.

"Yes, please. I am looking for a place to stay." I heard my voice as clipped and colourless by comparison with his.

"Ah! You are an American!"

"No, I'm Canadian," I said, sounding slightly defensive.

"Well, that's even better! Would you care to sign our overseas visitors' book?"

"Sure."

I hated signing those books. Who ever looked at them, anyway? Always the same polite, unimaginative scrawls wherever you went: "Beautiful scenery"; "We loved it"; "Very nice."

Kenner Elias Jones reached inside his blazer jacket, took out a gold fountain pen, uncapped it and handed it to me. It was elegant and nicely balanced. I paused for a brief moment to appreciate it then finished writing and pushed the book back across the counter. My script was easy to see on the page because the pen had a wide nib and was charged with turquoise ink.

Kenner inspected the page. "Oh, I see you're from British Columbia! You're an awfully long way from home, aren't you? And what's this? *K-l-a-how-ya Till-tillicum*? What the devil is that?"

"It's a west coast Native phrase that means 'Greetings, friend.' So there you go. Learn that and you'll be able to speak a Canadian language."

He practised it a few times. We both laughed.

I handed the pen back to him. "It's marvellous," I said. "The ink flows so easily it almost makes you want to sit and write."

"Thank you." Kenner smiled, carefully recapped the pen and tucked it back into his jacket. "It's very precious to me."

He recaptured my gaze and held my eyes a moment.

Then came the questions: Where was I going? Was I travelling by myself? How long would I be there? The conversation carried on while he made arrangements for my stay.

I asked him to book my room for a few nights. It would be nice to stay put for a while and explore. And I had found someone to talk to. Travelling alone had many rewards, but for me loneliness was something I hadn't expected.

I left Kenner to his other travellers after promising to come back and visit during the next few days. My budget was tight and my room was in the lowest price range. That meant getting the room key in the hotel lobby and lugging my pack up five floors by myself to a tiny room in the attic.

I opened the door and my aching arms gladly dumped my pack in a corner. It was always this way. When I would finally stop somewhere after a day of travelling, putting that pack down knowing I wouldn't have to pick it up again until the next day was like being let out of jail. Then I'd fall on my back on the bed and stare at the ceiling while I let the tiredness seep out of my shoulders and neck.

It was a good pack. I had shopped carefully for it before leaving Canada. It was made of orange waterproof canvas and had a strong but light internal aluminum frame. The shoulder straps and hip belt were wide and well padded. When properly adjusted, the hip belt bore most of the pack's weight. I had filled the pack completely and strapped a sleeping bag on the outside. When I wasn't wearing my straw sun hat, I would tie it to the top of the pack and it would swing gently behind.

My pack seemed to take on a personality of its own. It went everywhere with me; sat on my knee on buses and trains and beside me in restaurants. It endured being shoved, tugged and struggled with; it tolerated accusations of overweight and unmanageability with a stoic calm. It knew I wouldn't leave it behind. I laughed quietly to myself thinking about my silent companion. Earlier in the day I had stopped at a café for lunch. After being

shown to a table for two, I put my pack on the chair oppo-
site me, since it would be easier to pick up from there than
from the floor. Feeling particularly lonely, I took off my
straw hat and put it on the top of the pack. So my shape-
less, orange, chapeau-adorned lunch guest stared quietly
across the table at me as I ate my meal.

Once I had settled into my poky room in Llandudno
and rested a bit, I went back downstairs and outside to look
around. For three days I roamed the town, strolling the
promenade, breathing in the sea air and hiking up and
around the Great Orme.

Every afternoon I would visit Kenner in the tourist hut
on the promenade. At three he'd get a coffee break, and we
would walk over to a tea shop around the corner, drink
cups of strong tea, eat toasted tea buns and talk. He was a
wonderful conversationalist on a wide range of topics, and
was funny, intelligent and had a wealth of information
about Wales. It didn't take long for me to find I was looking forward to our visits. True, finding a friend relieved
the loneliness of solitary travel, but there was something
else. Although I had only just met him, Kenner felt like
someone I already knew.

The days vanished quickly, and in keeping with the itin-
erary I had set for myself, it was soon time to head north to
Scotland. Kenner tried to persuade me to stay longer, but
I wanted to get going. However, I did promise to stop by the
tourist hut upon my return to North Wales in a few weeks'
time. The Welsh National Eisteddfod was coming up and
would be held in Caernarfon, Kenner's hometown, about
twenty miles away. The Eisteddfod is the national festival of
literature, music, dance and other cultural performances. It

seemed an event not to be missed. Kenner tried to find me a place to stay in Caernarfon for that week, but all hotels and bed-and-breakfasts were booked.

"You can't come all this way and miss the Eisteddfod," Kenner said. "Come and stay for the week with me and Mother. She loves to have guests."

"Are you sure there is room?"

Kenner assured me there was then added, "It's only a small house. Nothing posh like you Canadians are used to."

We both laughed and I expressed my thanks. It appeared a generous, kind offer. I agreed to stop in Llandudno on my way back from Scotland. Off I went in the best of spirits.

After several weeks enjoying the highlands, lowlands and islands of Scotland, I returned to North Wales and once again found my way to the tourist hut in Llandudno. Kenner seemed genuinely happy to see me and rang up his mother to say their guest was on the way. He took out his gold pen and wrote some directions on a scrap of paper then handed the paper to me, smiling. "Don't get lost," he said, "or Mother will be frantic."

I left and found the bus heading south. The ancient vehicle wound its way through the byways and back roads to Bangor, Port Dinorwic and finally Caernarfon's town square.

The square was the terminus for all the local and regional buses. They came and went from long concrete islands under the watchful eye of a statue of David Lloyd George. Rows of shops ringed the open space. At one end was the imposing fortress of Caernarfon Castle. I wanted to stop and explore, but thinking someone would be expecting me, I took out the scrap of paper with Kenner's handwritten directions:

"Take the street that leaves the square and goes past the Castle Pharmacy. When you get to the department store, turn right and continue on until you come to Lon Ysgol—then Victoria Road, Pendalar to Cil Coed. Go left on Cil Coed, right on Caer Garreg. Watch for five concrete steps."

I had to ask for help along the way, but I soon found myself at the gate to the small garden of 11 Glan Peris, in a row of undistinguished houses. I didn't know what to expect when I reached the front door. What would this lady be like? Would she approve of me? Would I feel comfortable or want to get away? With my pack strapped on my back and my sun hat in my hand, I took a deep breath and knocked. There was no reply. I knocked again.

This time a voice called, "Come in—it's open."

I entered. "Hello?"

No answer, so I walked through the minuscule kitchen and into the not-much-larger sitting room. There on the sofa sat Kenner's mother, Primrose Elias Jones. She was a short, plump woman with large glasses, grey dishevelled hair, stubby brown shoes and a worn polyester dress. Tears were rolling down her face.

"I've been waiting for you to come. I just knew you'd come."

My pack still on my back, I sat down beside her and put my arms around her. Whatever was the matter?

"Mrs. Jones, what is it? Are you all right? Shall I call for someone?"

Confused, I sat there and held her. She cried for a few minutes like a heartbroken, tired child. Then she recovered.

"I'm sorry. That was no way to welcome a guest. I just had the feeling that you would be someone I could talk to, and I've been waiting for you all day. I'm so glad you're here. Let me make you a cup of tea and you can put your things over here . . ."

Primrose bustled about. She seemed to have collected herself for the moment, so I decided to let her explain herself in her own time. While she made tea, I looked around the room. It had a tiny coal fireplace, with an exceedingly sooty rug in front of it. A grimy yellow plastic bucket half filled with coal sat on the hearth. An alarm clock ticked loudly on the top of the television set. On the wall was a black-and-white photograph of Caernarfon's town square on a busy market day. Nearby was a picture of a school choir.

Orangey-brown curtains covered the window that overlooked the garden. Two birds were sitting on a clothesline strung between the house and the garden wall. An unruly fuchsia bush threatened to overwhelm every other plant nearby, but a few flowers and one rosebush appeared to be holding their own.

Primrose came back carrying a tray with a teapot, cups and saucers, milk, sugar and a plate of biscuits. As we sipped our tea, she asked me about my journey from Llandudno and whether I had been able to follow Kenner's directions.

"They were a bit confusing," I said. "I asked a few people along the way to make sure I was going in the right direction. The streets and signs are all in Welsh, so it was a challenge."

"Well, you're here," said Primrose. "And we're happy to have you."

At the front door, a dog whined and scratched. Primrose went through the house and opened the door to admit a small Sheltie. Timmy barked severely at me for a few minutes in spite of repeated admonishments. Eventually quiet returned, and Primrose began to explain why she had been in tears when I arrived.

Her life had been a hard one, she said. She had been left a widow when Kenner was only a few months old and had to raise him alone. "No one wanted to help me. And then he made a few mistakes, and people want to talk about him and tell stories, and it's hard to live in the town and put up with the things people say. Why don't they just leave us alone and let us live our own lives?"

I wasn't entirely sure what all this was about. But in keeping with my role as a listener, I decided she would explain in due time if she wanted to. I wasn't to know at that point that she was going to unburden her heart and tell me stories of her life, her marriage and her struggles to raise Kenner. For now, she settled on telling me about her sister, Arial.

She and Arial had left their family home in Devon for North Wales as young women. Primrose worked as a nurse and Arial as a secretary. Arial was diagnosed with Parkinson's disease and was looked after by her adoring sister until she died.

Primrose, weeping again, stopped to gather herself.

"The worst thing of all was Arial didn't even recognize me that last while before her death. And you know what? She never said thank-you for all the care I took of her for years and years. And when the undertaker came with the coffin, they put my sister in it and brought it down the stairs, but it was too big to go through the front door. Can you imagine that? Oh, it was different bringing it in. They didn't have the lid on and they could turn it sideways to get around the corners. But then when my poor sister was inside, they couldn't get it back out. They had to take the glass out of the window in the front room and then took the coffin through the window. I was horrified! That night I went to the meeting where the town council was, and I marched right in and I said to them that they had better smarten up when they build houses in this town. Because people not only have to live in them they have to die in them. I really told them, I did!"

Primrose dried her tears and took me upstairs to show me where I would be sleeping. There were three bedrooms and a bathroom. One bedroom was used for storage, the second was Kenner's and the third Primrose's. There were two single beds in Primrose's room. I was to sleep in one of them.

"I got these beds so that I could have Arial nearby me all the time." Primrose spoke in a quiet voice. "Before she got poorly, we would talk at night like schoolgirls. But when her condition got worse and worse, she used to get scared. In the night she would call out and reach across for me. I'd find her hand in the dark and hold on tight. And we'd lie there, holding hands between the beds until she fell asleep. I'd have to pry her fingers open to get my hand away."

I didn't know what to say. Primrose stood for a few seconds, lost in memories, and then stood up straighter and looked at me.

"I miss her dreadfully."

After stowing my pack in a corner, I followed her back downstairs. This was my first real look at the kitchen because I had come through it quickly when I entered the house. It seemed to me more like a hallway. It was dark and narrow, with a window at one end and a curtained doorway into the sitting room at the other end. A gas range took up a good deal of space against one wall. There was no refrigerator. The countertops were worn, scratched blue laminate and the cupboard fronts painted off-white. The ceiling and the walls were somewhat grimy. The floor was finished with blue tiles that had rarely, if ever, seen a good wash. It made me wonder what sort of upbringing Kenner had had. Had his childhood home been cozy, nurturing, happy?

I helped prepare a simple supper of grilled lamb chops, cauliflower with cheese sauce, and boiled potatoes. Everything was cooking nicely by the time Kenner arrived home around seven. Timmy heard him and was barking furiously before Kenner even unlatched the garden gate. As he came in the back door, Timmy went wild, yelping and frisking about. Kenner's cheery "Hello!" went almost unheard amid the racket. After giving Timmy a good roughing in the kitchen, he came through the curtain into the living room.

"Well, I see you made your way here safe and sound. Right, then, Mother, what do you think of our Canadian guest? I certainly can pick them, can't I?"

Primrose had cheered up considerably when Kenner appeared. He stood there smiling, rubbing his hands in a sort of washing motion, peering through his glasses.

"I see you have supper well and truly started, Mother. I'll look after it from here. You two ladies just sit there and enjoy yourselves."

A few minutes later he came back into the room with cutlery and napkins, which he distributed to us, then went back into the kitchen. He reappeared with two plates heaped with steaming food.

Once we were settled, he brought in his own plate and we ate. He asked about my journey to the house that day and then described the tourists who had visited the hut on the promenade in Llandudno. Nothing was said by me or by Primrose about the sad discussions of the afternoon. Instead she described our day as filled with pleasant conversation—a lovely opportunity to get to know each other. I followed her lead, since she was clearly making an effort to put the best face on things and not let on that she had been unhappy and telling me family stories.

After more chatting and some television, we all retired. I was tucked away in the bed that had belonged to Arial. Primrose made small talk after the lights were out, but I was exhausted and fell into a deep sleep as she spoke.

The first thing I heard the next morning was a knock on the bedroom door. Kenner came barging in while Primrose and I struggled into wakefulness. He was carrying two trays.

" 'Morning, ladies! Breakfast!"

I barely had time to boost myself into a sitting position before I found in front of me poached eggs on toast, bacon, a grilled tomato, orange juice, a cup of tea and a vase of flowers.

"I hope you like eggs. I took the chance that you would." He smiled at me, rubbing his hands as he had the previous night, head tilted to one side.

I assured him I did. He stayed with us for a few minutes as we chatted about the weather then left to catch the bus for Llandudno. While Primrose and I ate, I realized I felt as though I was in some kind of book where I was suddenly the centre of attention. I had never had someone get up early to make me breakfast in bed and then serve it with politeness and flourish. I felt special—but uncomfortable, too.

I spent a week in Caernarfon. A routine soon took shape. In the morning Primrose and I would bustle about, doing a bit of laundry, tidying up the place and deciding by eleven that it was certainly time for a cup of tea. Neighbours would come and go during the day. They would always be served tea and biscuits while they talked about whichever neighbour didn't happen to be there at the time. I was continually flooded with details and gossip about the townsfolk, debate about what to cook for supper and who was at the shops today and what they were buying.

One thing I found strange was that in all the endless conversations, Primrose's visitors asked very few questions of me. Here I was, having travelled almost halfway around the world, yet they seemed to have no curiosity about me at all. They magnified the drama and importance of the smallest details of their own lives. I wondered at one point if they were just following some code of politeness in not exploring my experiences and impressions. But they really didn't seem to care. I wasn't offended, just surprised.

I, on the other hand, enjoyed listening to them chatter in their wonderful lilting accent. In fact, instead of paying attention to what they were saying, I was fascinated with how they said it.

Another routine quickly emerged. Every day as soon as the chores were done, the neighbours had gone and quiet had settled in, Primrose would begin her stories. She had meant what she said. She did indeed see me as someone she could talk to. And when I thought about it, I could see why. I came from far, far away and had no connections with her and her history or any of the people involved. When I left, who would I possibly tell?

I felt badly for Primrose, who seemed so lonely and heartsore. No matter how frustrating it was at times I never interrupted or minimized what she was saying. I was a polite listener—the perfect audience. Never once did she reveal our conversations to Kenner. Instead she seemed to go to great lengths to pretend to him that everything was wonderful and she was perfectly happy. He would appear to believe her but perhaps was simply choosing to ignore the truth. I felt that by giving my time and attention as she told her stories, I was repaying her kindness in having me in her home. I found myself often just taking a deep breath and encouraging myself to be patient.

The very first morning after my arrival Primrose began.

"I was a nurse. And I loved being a nurse. My job was at the local sanatorium. That's where the tuberculosis patients were."

It was easy to imagine her as a young woman, dressed

in her perfectly pressed and starched uniform, making her way through the streets of Caernarfon with a quick and confident step.

"Medicine then wasn't what medicine is now," she continued. "Tuberculosis was common, and I was needed. I loved being needed. But I didn't want to marry." Primrose's voice shifted a few notes higher. "Arial and I just wanted to live together and neither of us wanted a husband. That was our plan."

But it didn't work out that way.

John Elias Jones was a tuberculosis patient at the sanatorium. When Primrose came to the door of the men's ward, she could see John's face light up.

"He'd say, 'Hello, Nurse Hawkins.' And when I said, 'Hello, John, how are you doing?' he would smile like a happy child and say, 'Much better, now that you are here, Nurse.' Ooooh, I told myself. Watch out."

Primrose tried to brush him off. "I hoped he wasn't entertaining any ideas about me," she said. "I couldn't possibly get involved with him. I didn't want a husband. I was much older than he was, anyway. And besides that, well, he just wasn't my type. He was tall and skinny and had huge ears and a mop of untameable hair. No, no, not for me."

Primrose sighed. "Eventually he got better and the doctor said he could go. I felt relieved. I thought that was the end of it."

The first day Primrose went to work after John Elias Jones had been discharged from the hospital, she got a surprise.

"I had finished my shift and was going home. When I came out the front door of the sanatorium, I couldn't believe my eyes. There, standing at the gate, was John, and I thought: Oh no." The expression on Primrose's face mirrored her feelings at the time—a combination of frustration and annoyance. "I took a deep breath and headed for the gate," she said. "I had no choice."

For a fleeting moment she thought, hoped, that John was there to see someone else. Not so. "'Hello, Nurse Hawkins,' he says to me. What cheek! I had done nothing to encourage this man. But no, no, he wasn't going to accept that." John said he would like to walk Primrose home. She tried to decline his offer, but he insisted. "What could I do? It's a free country. I couldn't stop him from walking where he wanted to." John saw Primrose to her door and then went to his own home, on Snowdon Street, where he lived with his mother and his brother William.

Life at the house on Snowdon Street turned out to be a story in itself. Primrose explained that the house was like so many of the old, original houses in Caernarfon, built of stone and cold masonry, the heating limited to coal fires. The darkened rooms with small windows could be chilly and airless.

According to Primrose, it was well known in town that it wasn't a happy home and commonly accepted that the source of the unhappiness was John and William's mother.

"Oh no," she said bitterly. "Who could possibly be happy living with the Old Dutch?"

I didn't interrupt to ask why Primrose called her that. Presumably it was derived from *Duchess*. Certainly it was uttered with pure dislike.

"She," Primrose said, "was a nasty, hard old woman.

She had five children. *Five!* But she didn't believe in doctors. Oh no. And when her children were sick, do you think she'd call for the doctor? Not a chance." Primrose paused, remembering; she was almost vibrating with outrage. "She always knew best. And for all that what happened? She let three—*three*—children die because she wouldn't let the doctor see them. She buried them and still believed she was right. She was stupid. Mad."

"So how was it that John was allowed into the sanatorium?"

"Well, by the time he was sick with tuberculosis, he was not a child anymore. She couldn't tell him what to do. So he came to the hospital. It saved his life. Don't think for a minute that the Old Dutch approved. But she had to bite her tongue. Stupid woman."

The Eisteddfod was being held in a vast tent in a farmer's field just outside the town. Kenner guided me around the grounds one day, taking me into some of the exhibition booths and translating for me, as only Welsh was spoken. I was overwhelmed by what I was seeing and hearing. What an adventure to wander about and see things that looked different, try new foods and listen to incomprehensible chatter. I loved it. Kenner was a perfect host and gentleman. He patiently explained the customs, recipes and some of the magic of the Welsh language. Being in his company was easy. I let myself imagine what it would be like if this was my home, my life.

When the day was over and supper finished back at Primrose's house, Kenner suggested we go for a walk. It was a rainy night, so we put on our waterproof jackets and went down through the town, past the castle and over the estuary to a park on the other side. We walked quietly in the rain for about an hour. I remember looking at him walking in front of me and wondering, as I had earlier that day, if I could see myself here, with this person. He wasn't physically attractive to me, but he was charming, intelligent, entertaining. So what was it that made me feel unsettled? I didn't know.

Kenner walked ahead of me in the dim light. His jacket was dark and slick, with water streaming in the folds of fabric. The pathway was soggy underfoot. Leaves on the trees dripped and shook with the weight of the raindrops. I suddenly realized I was damp and uncomfortable, and swamped with a feeling that I really did not want to be there. Right at that moment Kenner half turned to look back at me, not breaking his stride. His face was framed by the hood of his jacket. I could see his eyes and a half grin, a frightening, sly, conniving-looking smile. His eyes were empty. I felt as if he was checking to see if I was still there, within reach; as if he couldn't believe his luck, like a spider with a fly caught in its web. I didn't feel safe.

We kept walking. He glanced back several times again and looked at me with those unreadable eyes.

Relief washed through me when we left the wild area and got back into the town. Under the lights and in the street I wondered if my imagination had been running away with me. Perhaps I was being too dramatic, too harsh. Back home, with a hot cup of tea in hand and my feet warming by the coal fire, I tried to forget that face. But it surfaced in my thoughts throughout the evening, and each time it did, I cringed inside.

By morning the rainstorm had passed. A few herds of robust clouds were all that remained. The sun was fighting through—and winning. The day was new, the gardens refreshed. Clean morning air drifted through Primrose's home, chasing out the damp and the traces of smoke from the coal fire. In the presence of Primrose's cheerfulness and busy hustling and bustling I easily dismissed what I had seen and felt the night before.

As we gave the upstairs an airing, we went into the storage room. Primrose moved some books and a pile of sweaters from the top of an old trunk and lifted the lid. A stale scent testified to how long the trunk had been undisturbed. She reached in and took out a stack of photographs.

"Look! Good Lord, I haven't seen these in ages," she said. She sat on a nearby box and indicated a chair for me. "Well, well, hmm." She passed me an old photograph enclosed in a stiff paper frame. "My wedding day," she said quietly.

"This is lovely," I said, looking at the image in pastels and soft greys.

"Yes."

Primrose sighed. I waited. After looking away to collect her thoughts, she told me how she came to be in that picture.

"After John waited for me at the hospital gate," she said, "I was expecting it to be just a one-time thing." Her mouth firmed in annoyance. "Oh no. Every day when I came out from work, there he was, waiting for me.

"Didn't you tell him to not come to walk you home?" I asked.

"I did! I certainly did. I told him he should not waste his time with me. That I was not interested in going out with him or anything. But he would not be put off. Oh, and don't think for a moment that the town didn't start to talk. Of course, suddenly Primrose was the centre of gossip. Why can't people just mind their own business?"

As she continued her story, I learned that not only did the townspeople feel free to comment but so, too, did John's mother.

"The Old Dutch absolutely hated the idea that John was walking with me," Primrose said. "First of all, I was part of the medical world—and she wouldn't have anything good to say about that. And like I told you, I was much older than John. She was right about that, and I agreed that he should find someone his own age. Nothing doing. John wouldn't hear of it.

"The Old Dutch thought I was weaving my web around John against his will. As if that were the truth! I told him not to come to the gate. But he wouldn't listen. And then one day he told me he wanted to marry me." She sighed again. "I had been hoping all along that his attentions were merely those of a lonely man needing conversation. But oh no. So I decided I would have to be blunt."

Primrose described how she drew herself up to her full four-foot-ten and looked him straight in the eyes.

"I said, 'John, you have done me a great honour, but I must refuse you. I have no intention of marrying you or anyone else. I am too old for you, anyway. Go and find a nice girl your own age. I am sorry, but if this is how you feel, we cannot see each other again. Goodbye.' And then I turned and walked away."

"But he didn't listen to you, did he?"

Primrose laughed. "No, he certainly did not. The next day he was at the gate again. He pursued me for five years. *Five years!* He wore me down," she said.

When John asked her again to marry him, Primrose repeated her answer. "But this time it was different," she said "This time when I turned him down, he had tears in his eyes. He said that if I didn't marry him, then he would have no chance. He said no one else would have him and he would be condemned to living a long, lonely life." Primrose looked down at her hands then back up at the open door. "So I took pity on him. I know it was a mistake, but I felt as though I would be ruining this man's life if I didn't marry him. I had been raised to consider the happiness of others before my own, and that thinking only of myself was being selfish. So I said yes, even though I didn't love him—I only pitied him."

Primrose and John were married at a registry office in Caernarfon. The new couple left the office and walked the few blocks to the photographer's studio. The camera captured a picture of the day Primrose Hawkins wed John Elias Jones. I looked down again at the photograph in my hands. There John stands in his dark suit and starched white shirt, his tie tight up against his throat. Lanky, with cropped dark hair and huge ears sticking out. His eyes smiled into narrowness; his wide mouth stretched into a grin. His bony arms hung by his sides, one bent to support the arm of his new wife.

And there next to him is a young, sweet-faced Primrose. Small, round, soft. Her dress is made from light fabric in a gentle shade of blue. Her belt, hat, gloves and shoes are a rich maroon red. Her mouth is smiling, but her eyes are not.

The next photograph was another wedding picture. "That's Will and Katie," Primrose explained. "John's brother. I told you he was blind? Well, so was his wife. Katie could see only a little bit. She'd go out about the town carrying a big umbrella, rain or shine. When she wanted to cross the street, she would wave it in front of her like a sword." Primrose laughed, and I joined her as I imagined the sight. "Yes. She was quite a personality. But they were happy together."

Primrose made another selection from the small pile of photographs.

"I have always loved this one so much," she said, handing me a miniature black-and-white of a mother and child.

I looked closely. Primrose was holding to her a small boy, their heads together. His curls dark and his eyes big; her smile this time soft and genuine. Kenner and Primrose.

"He was a lovely boy," she said. "But it is so sad that his father never had a chance to see him grow up."

"How did that happen?" I asked.

Primrose put the picture down and placed her plump hands on her knees, as if bracing herself for the next part of the story.

"When we married, we went to live in the house on Snowdon Street. I really didn't want to, but there wasn't enough money in our bank account for a house of our own, so we had to live with the Old Dutch."

That grim, tight-lipped look was back on Primrose's face.

"Well, we had to make the best of it."

Before long, Primrose was pregnant. "There I was, thinking that at nearly forty I was too old to have a baby," she said. "But when I realized I might be expecting, I took myself right over to Dr. Griffiths' surgery. After he did an exam, he waited for me in his office. I walked in and sat down. I can still see his face. He lifted himself out of his chair and reached across, offering to shake my hand. He said, 'Well, my dear, you are indeed pregnant. My heartiest congratulations!'

"It suddenly just seemed that it had all been worth it—being married when I didn't really want to be then having to live under the same roof as the Old Dutch."

Primrose left the surgery and went to sit down by the castle, in a quiet corner.

"I sat in the sunshine for a long time. I felt warm and happy. But of course a baby would change everything."

"Of course. How could it not?" I said.

"Yes, well, John was very happy with the news. But the Old Dutch wasn't so sure. John said he now had a family to support and needed work. So he tried to find a job in town, but there just wasn't anything."

Primrose stayed at her nursing as long as she could, and John went to London to look for work. "That left me alone in the house with the Old Dutch," she said. "I just tolerated her as best I could. After all, once the baby came, surely we would be able to find a place of our own."

She had a month to go in her pregnancy when the labour pains began. John was still in London. Primrose was rushed to hospital in nearby Bangor, where after many hours she gave birth to a tiny, thin boy. The pain and the effort nearly did her in. She was unconscious when her baby took his first breath and cried in Dr. Griffiths' arms. He put the baby into special care and left instructions to be called immediately at any sign of difficulty. Then he turned to his patient. Primrose was still asleep when she was rolled back into her room on the maternity ward.

"When I woke up, the first person I saw was Dr. Griffiths. What a kind man. Right away he said, 'Primrose, my dear, you have a little boy.' I wanted to see my baby. Where was he? And what about John? Did he know he had a son? Dr. Griffiths explained that they were trying to get in touch with John now and told me not to worry. But how could I not? I'm a nurse. I knew the baby was very early and might not be healthy. But the doctor said that although my baby was quite small, he seemed to be fine."

Primrose longed to see her boy, but Dr. Griffiths wouldn't allow it. He explained that the baby couldn't be moved until they knew he was strong enough, and Primrose needed to recover before she could go to the ward in which he was being cared for.

When she was declared well enough to travel down the hall, she could only look through a window at her baby.

"He was such a tiny, tiny thing. A puckered face. His skin was blotchy. He weighed only four and a half pounds."

Primrose was bursting to hold him but could only look. "Be patient," I told myself. "He has to grow. He has to survive." She was wheeled back to her room.

After several more days of recovery, the doctor said Primrose was well enough to go home. So, with her suitcase in her hand, she trudged up Snowdon Street to the house. She had left her son in the care of the nursery staff at the hospital; he wasn't yet strong enough to leave. But John was now home, and only learned on his arrival that he had a son. He had come home because the tuberculosis had returned and his lungs were racked with pain like never before. Once he walked through the door of the house on Snowdon Street, he never left.

Kenner was so frail the doctor said he couldn't risk vaccinating him against tuberculosis, and until he was strong enough for that, he couldn't be sent home. For a whole month the baby was kept in the hospital, and Primrose was not allowed to go near him in case she carried a trace of the infection with her. "It nearly killed me," she said. "He was my child and I couldn't hold him. I could only see him through the glass."

The weeks went by as Primrose took care of John at home and Kenner slowly grew bigger and more robust in the hospital.

Eventually Dr. Griffiths said Kenner was well enough to leave.

"I went right up to the ward and picked him up," she said. "At long last, I had my baby in my arms." Primrose returned with him to Snowdon Street. "And can you believe it? There in the hallway was the Old Dutch. She looked at Kenner, and strange as it sounds, her face changed. I had this funny feeling she thought it was her own baby and she wanted to take him from me. But nothing doing. I just pushed past her and headed up the stairs. John was waiting to see his son."

Primrose walked into the bedroom and placed Kenner beside John. "He was too weak to pick him up. He just smiled and looked at him. Then he rubbed the baby's cheek with his finger, gently, slowly. He looked up at me and said, 'Thank you, Primrose, for giving me this beautiful boy.'"

Kenner was barely three months old when his father died. The old woman buried John next to her other three children.

Through the rest of the week, Primrose continued to bring out her stories. They were prompted each time by the memories tucked away in the upstairs room.

"Would you mind going up and getting the pictures?" she asked one morning over the rim of her teacup.

Off I went, wondering as I mounted the stairs what I was going to hear this day. I reminded myself that I was a guest in her home. Although I wanted to escape, I felt I couldn't be impolite.

When I returned, Primrose shuffled through the photographs a moment and took out one of a very young Kenner, cheeky smile, curly hair. Charming.

"Oh, how sweet," I said.

Primrose smiled. "Yes, he was a lovely boy. And so smart," she said. "The Old Dutch looked after him while I went to work." Primrose and Kenner were now forced to stay with the old lady, as there was really no other way. "I went back to nursing, and as a single mother I needed her help to take care of Kenner. So I worked during the day and she would mind him. Then I would take over when I came home." Primrose explained that Kenner's grand-mother was very strict with him and wouldn't let him go and play with other children or have any little friends come to the house on Snowdon Street. "The poor tyke spent a lot of time alone with her and on his own in his room," she said. "So I would take him out as much as I could. But I'm afraid he was pretty lonely."

Primrose paused in her storytelling to gather herself. I just waited.

"Then one day something horrible happened," she said, taking a deep breath and looking out the window into the distance. "I was at work and I wasn't feeling well, so the doctor on duty said I should just take the rest of the day off."

Primrose walked home through Caernarfon and down Snowdon Street several hours ahead of her usual time. It was a warm, sunny day. The front door of the house was open to let in the fresh air. She mounted the steps without making a sound. "I wasn't trying to be silent," she explained. "But I was wearing my nursing shoes. They are very quiet." As she was passing through the hall, she noticed the door to the front room was open. The room was seldom, if ever, used. The good furniture was carefully protected with dust covers, ready for friends and guests who never came. Primrose, still in the hallway, glanced in.

"I couldn't believe my eyes!" she exclaimed.

"What?" I said.

Primrose looked at me, that now-familiar expression of disapproval on her face and went on.

"There was a table in the centre of the room with a clean white cloth on it. Kenner was standing in the middle of the table, motionless. Primrose's voice went up an octave and she was speaking quickly. "And he was wearing old clothes, old clothes that had belonged to John when he was a boy. They weren't Kenner's things—they were his father's. And there—there was the Old Dutch." Primrose wrung her hands in her lap, recalling the scene. "Yes, there she was, walking slowly, slowly around the table, looking at Kenner. No, not just looking at him. The only way I can describe it was she was *worshipping* him!" Primrose exhaled with force. "I didn't know what to do," she said. "I knew it was wrong. So wrong. So horrid. What was she doing with my boy? I wanted to rush in there and carry him away and run, run, run from that crazy old woman. But where would I go?"

Primrose explained that in those days there was no community help for a single parent. I could see the dilemma.

"I had no family here except Arial, and she lived in a very small place." Primrose was trapped.

With a resigned look on her face now, she described how she quietly backed away from the door and out of the house. She walked to the castle, in turmoil, and sat on a bench. She turned the situation over and over in her mind. Was the old woman mad? Primrose had always thought so. The Old Dutch kept herself and everyone else on a very tight rein. She never laughed, never seemed to relax, never found joy in the simple pleasures of life. Yet there was no other place for Primrose to live.

"I was frightened and angry and I just couldn't see a way out," she said.

It was a lonely and helpless Primrose who sat in the shadow of the castle through the rest of the afternoon. Then, at her usual time of arrival, she returned to the house on Snowdon Street. As she walked into the hall, she saw the door to the front room was once again closed. She said nothing.

One of Primrose's closest friends was a sweet, dithering, gentle soul named Ruby. She would regularly present herself at the door without warning, calling out in Welsh as she came into the kitchen, "Hello, hello, it's me, Ruby."

"*Dewch i mewn!* Come in!" Primrose would respond, her face lighting up at the sight of her friend.

Ruby couldn't resist dropping by almost every day to inspect the visitor from far away. I suspect I was the subject of many a neighbourly gossip elsewhere. That didn't worry me at all. Besides, I spent as much time observing Ruby as she did observing me.

She was a widow in her early sixties, quiet, unassuming, almost afraid to speak. Ruby never offered her thoughts or opinions unless asked, and then would only respond in very quiet tones and short sentences and agree with everything that was said. But every once in a while a glimmer of her personality would show through.

"Doesn't your mother miss you, being away so long?" she asked me.

"Well, yes," I answered. "But I call her every week to let her know that I'm okay. And I send letters," I explained.

"Mmm."

Ruby clearly didn't think that was enough.

"Primrose used to miss Kenner terribly when he went to visit his uncle John, Primrose's brother," she said.

"Oh, of course!" Primrose said, joining in. "But it was so good for him to get away and have some fun."

"Where was Uncle John?" I asked.

"In Barry," said Primrose. "He has a farm there. And in the summer Kenner would go there for a few weeks and have a holiday. I would miss him terribly, but I knew it did him a world of good."

"Tell her about the bull," Ruby prompted.

Primrose laughed and turned to me. "Be a dear and get the photographs from upstairs, and I'll tell you."

Off I went. After I returned with the pictures and handed them to Primrose, she selected a black-and-white photo. She laughed as she handed it over.

Gazing out at me from the image was a gangly boy standing in a farmyard beside a black bull. Two men are in the background, one appearing to enjoy the scene immensely.

"Is this Kenner?" I asked.

"It is," Primrose replied. "It was a source of endless amusement on that farm how that bull, Billy, just loved Kenner."

It seems that Kenner had been visiting one summer and couldn't be found when Uncle John went to look for him.

Ruby couldn't resist. "And you'll never, ever guess where—"

"I'm telling the story!" Primrose slapped her hands on her knees and shot her friend a piercing glance.

"Oh, sorry, Prim." Ruby sat back in her chair.

Primrose picked up the story. "Uncle John checked the barn. He checked the sheds, the house. Kenner was nowhere." Then it occurred to him to look in the very last place he thought Kenner could possibly be. "He told me he didn't for a single moment think it was worth checking the field where Billy was, but he had searched everywhere else. And what do you think? There was Billy, lying peacefully in the sunshine. And there, fast asleep with his head on the bull's belly, was Kenner. Uncle John was dumbfounded. Billy never let anyone come near him." Primrose laughed again. "When Uncle John called and Kenner woke up, he just patted his friend Billy on the head and came over to see what his uncle wanted. Uncle John said he'd never seen the beat of it, before or since."

Ruby smiled and shook her head, amazed all over again. "That bull remembered him every year," she said. "Every year. Isn't that right, Prim?"

"That's right." Primrose was smiling. "He would go and visit Billy when his chores were done. He would talk to that bull, even read to him." She shook her head, still smiling. "Billy never would let anyone else into his field. Oh no. He'd stamp and snort and charge. No, only Kenner."

Except for a few visits to the Eisteddfod with Kenner, I spent most of my time with Primrose. I thought I had heard all the stories, but not quite. Another item emerged from the trunk. It was a book that looked like a ledger. On the cover was hand printed the title: *Doomsday Book*.

"Take a look inside," said Primrose "You will never see anything like it. It's Kenner's book."

I ran my hand over the cover, wondering why he had chosen this name. I remembered my history from school. In the eleventh century William the Conqueror, the first Norman king of England, commissioned the *Domesday Book*. It was a listing of landowners in England and parts of Wales, their assets and estimated worth, compiled so

Index from Kenner's "Doomsday Book".

King William's officials could calculate taxes. Because the *Domesday Book* was a permanent record, people began to compare it to the Book of Life mentioned in the Bible, which would be placed before God on Judgment Day, otherwise known as Doomsday.

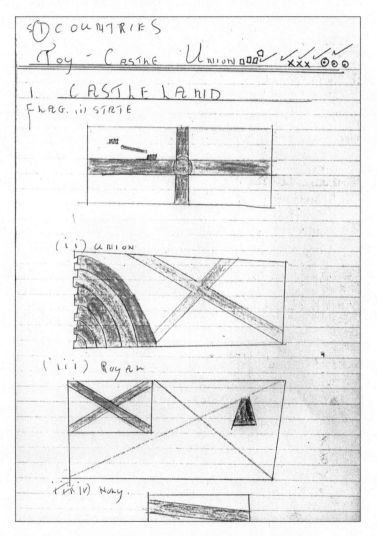

"Castle Land" flags from Kenner's "Doomsday Book".

I opened Kenner's *Doomsday Book*. Page after page was filled with hand-drawn maps of fantasy countries with names like Castleland, William Land and WetPuddle. Each map had cities, towns and geographical features. To the side of each map Kenner had noted the kind of government in place in each country—republic or constitutional monarchy—and which political party was in power. After slowly examining some of the pages, I looked up at Primrose. "What is this all about?"

"He started it the year I got scarlet fever," she said. "It was summer and Kenner was all ready to go to Uncle John in Barry, when I came down sick. So, so sick. Dr. Griffiths said he wasn't even sure I would survive. But do you think for a moment that the Old Dutch would help? Not on your life. She said Kenner had to stay home to take care of me."

"Oh no," I said. "How awful."

"I was so ill I didn't even know what was going on," she said. "And poor Kenner was bitterly disappointed. Imagine— having to give up his special holiday to stay home and take care of me. But to be fair, he did. And I survived."

Primrose explained that while he was stuck in the house, Kenner decided to create a world of his own. "He was always interested in politics and government doings. I don't know where that came from, but he was. And there had just been an election here. He'd heard a speaker describing how a person or events could persuade voters to swing one way or the other. He thought this was a fascinating idea."

So while Primrose was wrestling her way to recovery, Kenner was sitting in his room, deciding the outcomes of imaginary elections. "He used to take sheets of blank paper

and then open his book to one of the countries he created," she continued. "Then he would run a campaign.
Kenner would begin with an existing set of numbers showing the imaginary standings of various political parties
and then factor in the elements that would cause voters to
swing—change their allegiances. Persuasive politicians,
natural disasters, unforeseen economic events—all would
come into play. He'd fill the blank paper with calculations
and somehow, in his own way, arrive at a result, and a
new government would be in power in a corner of his
make-believe world.

"I didn't really understand it all," said Primrose. "But he
would sit up there for hours. When I was well enough to get
out of bed, I'd come in to see what he was doing. He wouldn't
even hear me enter the room. He'd be totally absorbed."

I handed the strange book back to her.

"He went on to work in politics," she said. Here. Look at
these." Primrose leafed through the *Doomsday Book* to the
back and took out some folded newspaper cuttings.

"He made a name for himself," she said, handing them
to me.

The first cutting carried the headline "The shy student
who inspired a Liberal revival." The report was written by
Paul Potts:

> When someone masterminds six municipal
> election victories out of eight for the Liberals,
> it's worth noting. And when you realize this
> ballot-box 'general' is just 20 years old, then

you really have to sit up and take notice. The shy student gave the impression he was a trembling 16-year-old not long past the model trains stage. But beneath this astonishing exterior is an ice-cool brain capable of daunting organisation and tenacious campaigning.

In a by-election the previous month, Kenner as an election agent had apparently turned a "chaotic" Liberal campaign in Sheffield's Burngreave ward into a victory. As a result of his efforts the first Liberal since 1919 was elected to city council.

Potts wrote that "the future in the Liberal Party looks bright for Ken Jones." But Kenner was cautious in his response: "The Liberal Party happens to agree with most of what I believe; but the electorate must always come first and the party second. I shall have to take things slowly and see what develops."

"Wow, quite a success story," I said, returning the papers to Primrose, who tucked them back into the *Doomsday Book*.

"Yes," she agreed. "But I don't think it was a good thing. He was very talented at helping people get elected. But he changed somehow. I didn't understand why he wanted to be with those people. But he did."

She passed the *Doomsday Book* to me. "Be a dear and take that upstairs for me," she said. "These old bones are a bit tired today."

As I put the book away in the chest, one last stack of documents caught my eye. On the top was an envelope addressed to K. E. Jones, Esq., 11 Glan Peris. I picked it up. The paper was high quality, creamy and smooth.

Expensive. The writing was elegant, done with a fountain pen in a confident hand. I was curious—but not bold enough to examine the contents without permission. I decided to take the envelope and the documents down to Primrose.

"I hope you don't mind, but I saw these," I said, handing everything to her. Primrose smiled. "Not at all. Read this."

She slid a single sheet of letter paper out from inside the envelope, unfolded it and gave it to me: "The Earl Marshal presents his compliments and requests that you take note of the enclosed detailed instructions," the letter began.

"What is this about?" I asked.

Primrose smiled proudly. "He was asked to be part of the investiture of Prince Charles as Prince of Wales. What an honour! Very few people were part of that ceremony, and my boy was there. Let the town gossips talk about *that*!"

Primrose paused as I continued to read the letter and the instructions for the ceremony. The Queen and Charles and other dignitaries would be coming into the centre grounds of Caernarfon Castle. Preceding Charles into the castle would be a group called the "Representatives of the Churches: the President of the Free Church Council of Wales, the Most Reverend Gwilym Owen; the Auxiliary Bishop of Menevia, the Right Reverend L. D. Fox; the Bishop of Bangor, the Right Reverend G. O. Williams; the Archbishop of Cardiff, the Most Reverend J. A. Murphy, and the Archbishop of Wales, the Most Reverend W. G. H. Simon." A young woman named Margaret Helen Parry was to carry a Bible. Ahead of them all, carrying a cross: Kenner E. Jones.

I was impressed. "Kenner carried the cross in the ceremony?"

OFFICE FOR THE INVESTITURE OF THE PRINCE OF WALES
27/28 Northumberland Avenue, London W.C.2
Telephone OI-839 5181

The Earl Marshal presents his compliments
and requests that you take note of the enclosed
detailed instructions.

17th June 1969

Herald of Arms
The Cross
borne by
Kenner E. Jones

The Bible
borne by
Miss Margaret Helen Parry

President of the Free Church Council of Wales
The Most Reverend Gwilym Owen

Auxiliary Bishop of Menevia   Bishop of Bangor
Right Reverend L. D. Fox   Right Reverend G. O. Williams

Archbishop of Cardiff   Archbishop of Wales
Most Reverend J. A. Murphy   Most Reverned W. G. H. Simon

"It was a proud day."

"He certainly did." Primrose smiled. "And you can go right down to Caernarfon Castle and see for yourself," she said. "There's a display there and you'll see his picture. It was a proud day, I don't mind saying."

That afternoon I went for a walk by myself and explored the castle. The display, as Primrose had said, was there. A thin, serious, bespectacled young Kenner, dressed in church vestments, carries a tall processional cross through the town into the castle and then sits with the other church represent- atives in a grouping near the dais. While Kenner sat close by, the Queen completed the ceremony. Charles received a sword, a coronet, mantle, gold ring and gold rod and formally became the Prince of Wales.

Four thousand spectators watched and listened inside the castle walls. Thousands more congregated outside the fortress. Millions tuned in to the television and radio broadcasts.

I wandered through the castle grounds, imagining the day, the ceremony and the impact it must have had on a young man.

That evening when Kenner arrived home from work, I asked him about the experience.

"Yes," he said. "It was quite an honour. But you've seen the pictures in the castle. There isn't much more to say." He got up and went into the kitchen.

Primrose and I just looked at each other.

That night as I went to sleep I pondered my confusion. How was it that a man who apparently was talented in the world of political campaigning, and honoured by his church, was working a summer job in the Tourist Office in Llandudno? Oh well. As I had done often in this week of visiting, I dismissed the question from my thoughts.

When the time came for me to leave Caernarfon, I was secretly relieved: I'd had all I could manage of Primrose's sad stories. She cried as she stood by the garden gate, watching me walk away. Kenner smiled and waved. With my pack on my back, I turned one last time and wondered if I would ever see them again.

CHAPTER 2

Love Letters

I was back in my little apartment in Vancouver and in my second year of broadcast journalism at the British Columbia Institute of Technology. What a great relief to be home. I hadn't realized how homesick I was; how I'd yearned to see family, friends and familiar surroundings. Now that I was home and safe, Britain again became a place that was far away. Everyone wanted to hear about my travels and adventures. Time and distance only embellished the memories and stories.

A few weeks after I returned, a letter arrived from Kenner. I had a flashback to our first meeting in the tourist hut in Llandudno. The letter was written with the same fountain pen he had handed me to sign the visitors' book with, and in the same turquoise ink:

> *Hello! Well how are you after your stay with us mad British? As your plane was due to take off, I was reminded of that well-known saying, 'Farewells*

are the skin on the rice pudding of life'. How moving, don't you think?

I am now looking across Llandudno Promenade. There are very few people here. The change is truly stunning, as the man said when he was hit on the head by five pounds' worth of pennies. I'm looking forward to finishing here next Wednesday. It's so quiet, I've got nothing better to do than to write you letters.

I am going to leave the rest of the letter to Mother to write, so I'll say farewell for now. Just remember . . . yes just, Kenner

Attached was another letter, from Primrose, detailing a trip to the hairdresser to have a perm, and the menu for dinner that day.

I wrote a reply right away. When Christmas rolled around, I sent some packets of maple sugar—a very Canadian gift—along with Christmas cards. I received a card from the two of them. As a rule, I am not diligent at keeping up my end of a written correspondence, and when no more letters arrived from Wales, I, too, left off writing.

School had finished and I was working at my new job far away in Halifax, Nova Scotia, when my mother called to say a letter for me had arrived at her address in Nanaimo on Vancouver Island. I hadn't let Kenner and Primrose know my new location, so they had sent it to the only address they had. I asked her to open the letter and read it to me.

Neither of us was prepared for the contents:

You will be surprised to see the address from which this letter is sent. I am in prison. Don't collapse with laughter, please. I am quite serious. I borrowed some money from friends before Christmas, and they made a criminal complaint as I didn't pay them back straight away. The result is that I am behind bars and, as yet, I don't know how long for.

Mother's fridge blew up in November and I have been paying her coal, electricity and phone bills as well. By Christmas I'd run out of money. So, for the sake of about three hundred pounds, I'm here. Not to worry, it will all work out in the end. It could be called a human experience, a man of the world's look into the nether reaches of humanity. I'll get you to do a scoop on that when I get out. Only, it's cost me a lot—my job, my good name, a criminal record. And I'll be 30 in May, so a job won't be easy to come by.

Enough of that! If you still want to communicate with a criminal, then write care of home. Don't labour the matter if you write to Mother. She is pretty upset about it all, naturally. If you seal your letter to me inside hers, that should reach me okay.

My next letter will be more newsy.

All my love, Kenner

Mum and I could hardly believe what he'd written. I felt quite badly for Kenner. It seemed as though his best efforts had led him into an innocent mistake. Mum and I agreed it would be kind to write to him, as the days would undoubtedly crawl by in prison. Every letter I sent was immediately answered.

"My dear Friend," his next one started:

What a nightmare. Yes, I do feel 'shafted' and let down. However, one learns from one's mistakes and from now on I shall neither be so trusting nor so gullible. I hope it is needless for me to say that I did nothing which profited me a penny. I was trying to help a friend and in so doing went beyond my own means. I borrowed, and knowing that I could not borrow to lend to my friend, I uttered a false story so as to raise money from other colleagues. They got wind of the situation, my friend did a runner and I got left holding the baby. Result—I am here now until next January at the earliest, July at the latest.

Learning one's lesson is harsh, it seems. So is English law.

Mother seems okay, though as I am over 150 miles away she cannot visit me, particularly as I am in an 'open' prison miles out in the country. I know she is finding money tight and I am worried about her.

Most mail is not censored here, though they do read a specimen number of outgoing letters.

There are 400 men here and it is a prison for trusted and non-dangerous men. There are no walls or fences. We live in billets of 28 men, though I have my own room. It is an old army camp and has extensive playing fields, a gym, etc. I am one of the four cook/bakers. I work 5:30 to 1:00 and 3:30 to 6:00 seven days a week for 3 pounds 15 pence. In my spare time I attend German classes twice a week, I walk a lot, play badminton and chess, read, and occasionally look at television.

I have the Times and the Economist, so I keep in touch with world events.

My greatest headache is knowing where to look for work on my release. Unemployment is a major national problem, and the stigma of a prison sentence will not help much.

What, only one inch of paper left? I have oodles left to say. I'll buy another letter with a precious 14 pence next week on condition that you write by return mail. The address is on the reverse hereof.

Lots of love, Kenner

I grew up in an often tense and unhappy home. In many ways, we were a dysfunctional family. My father was an alcoholic. My mother, with five children around her, did her best to keep the family together, but she didn't have much in the way of time and energy to give to us individually. If my father cared about us, he didn't really know how to show it. I craved love and tenderness. I longed for loving arms around me and someone telling me I was cherished.

So as I came into adulthood, like so many others I had never been helped with this old wound. I didn't know how to identify what I had needed for so long. I didn't know how to see how my yearning for love and stability influenced my choices, not always for the better. Then along came Kenner. As I write this now, I admit to how difficult it has been to go back and reread my letters to him. I feel embarrassed by my naked naïveté and what can only be described as my efforts to persuade Kenner that I was worthy of more than friendship.

I see how I didn't think through or analyze my actions in any way. I just reacted. Somewhere in my thoughts and heart, I saw an opportunity to matter to someone and I pounced on it. My half of our correspondence began as just a chatty friendship with the goal of hoping to relieve the tedium for a person behind bars. But as the months went by, my longing for affection, stability and a family of my own coloured everything I wrote.

My pages are filled with unquestioning acceptance of whatever Kenner told me. My ability to brush aside any doubts or concerns was in fine working order. I led myself into dangerous territory. So after Mum and I talked about that first letter from prison and caught up on family news, I hung up the phone and sat and pondered. The idea of Kenner spending countless days without freedom was a terrifying to me. I believed him, of course, and had no reason not to, feeling badly for a friend who seemed the victim of an innocent, well-intended mistake.

What occurred to me much later was how I didn't notice or question the difference in his explanations of how he came to be charged. In the first letter he said he had borrowed money because of Primrose's household difficulties. In the second he said he had borrowed to help a friend. But none of that registered with me. The only thing on my mind was how I could help a person in distress.

Over the coming months the envelopes with British postage came in a steady stream:

Last week I had to end my letter somewhat abruptly due to lack of space. So here is Part II of the Kenner Jones Saga. At least it would be Part II if I could remember what I included in Part I. There may thus be some repetition.

I remember telling you about this place, but did I tell you that I shall be here for another six months to a year?

Why so long you may ask. I have asked that many times. To start with my sentence is not long by British standards. There are men in here serving eighteen months for traffic offences.

Secondly, I have had a previous brush with the law. In 1974 I overspent on an election and, as parliamentary agent for the candidate in question, thus contravened the Corrupt and Illegal Practices Act 1889, and the Representation of the Peoples' Act 1946 as amended in 1964. So you see, I am a recidivist! Shades of a Welsh Watergate, what!

Thus ends last week's letter. I will write this week's this week and in it reply to the letter of yours last week, which was in reply to mine of the week before last and which arrived this week.

Till next week, pray for me.

Your ever loving friend, Kenner

I was not surprised to hear about the risks run by a parliamentary agent. Not long before, I had flirted with the idea of involving myself in partisan politics and had attended an organizational meeting in advance of an upcoming election. There I had heard serious warnings about how dimly the courts looked upon any candidate's agent who overspent in a campaign. It was an easy mistake for an agent to make— as I understood it, even one dime over the limit could mean a conviction. I found it quite easy to dismiss this infraction of Kenner's and considered it no further, especially as I assumed he had only been sanctioned or fined.

In his next letter, Kenner made it clear he was despondent about his future. With almost two million unemployed in the UK, who would want to offer a job to what he described as "a smart-alec ex-con"? He said he felt all the good times lay behind him. Most of his former friends and colleagues were shunning him. Only his mother, me and a few acquaintances were willing to stand by him:

> *What do I do, my good old trusty friend? Where did*
> *I go wrong? I tried to do 'good works'. I enjoy hard*
> *work and I get on well with people. I try to be a*
> *pleasant guy. So now I'm kicked in the solar plexus*
> *and I don't know if this time I can pick myself up . . .*
> *again. I've picked myself up after previous downhill*
> *runs, but this one just about beats me. For the first*
> *time in my life, I must admit that I want help. I need*
> *to see a future for myself.*
>
> *Also, you said earlier that you would help if you*

could. Can you help Mother to make ends meet until I get out of this hell-hole? If you can't, don't worry. Just, please God, don't you stop writing as well. I do care for you a hell of a lot, you know.

See you soon, Kenner

I cried after I read that letter. He sounded so trapped and so depressed and without hope. Before he went to prison, he had been giving money to Primrose, as she lived on pension money and in council-sponsored housing. So beginning that day, I sent her twenty pounds every payday, which came to about a hundred dollars a month in Canadian currency. I also tried to bolster Kenner's spirits:

Well, Kenner, I finally got the last letter that went to Mum's. The serious letter. The one in which you say you're a failure. Serious stuff. I know that you are in better spirits now, and that letter was written some time ago, but now that I have it in my hands I want to make a comment: please don't ever think you can't write to me about how you are feeling. Go ahead and get it out of your system.

A failure? No. I believe in you, Kenner. You're not a loser. You may be down, but you're not out. You tell me whatever is on your mind. It matters to me. I love to get your letters.

After I wrote that line, I stopped and reread it. I realized it was true. I was an important person in this man's world.

I wrote as regularly as he did, but sometimes letters were delayed in the mail. In his next letter he asked, "Why don't you write? If it was my last letter and its final couple of paragraphs which offended thee, let my pen be struck dry and my nib wither and be banished to the uttermost depths."

I loved the fun and creative way he wrote to me. It was unusual, corny, but an effort to be entertaining. I was flattered that he would go to the trouble:

> *Mother is coming to visit me on August 21st, an occasion which promises to be something of an emotional one. Funnily enough, it is only since I came to prison that I have begun to get in touch with my emotions. In the past, for the most part, I forced myself to be as ignorant of my emotions as I could be. You must advise me on such matters.*
>
> *Strange as it may sound, I find it easier to put my thoughts and feelings to paper to you than to anyone else I know. Perhaps it is because I feel that we are quite alike in many ways. We are both grossly too jealous of our independence and perhaps a bit lonely as a result?*
>
> *For now, it's hail and farewell!*
>
> *God be with you. Kenner*

In his next letter, he carried on in the same vein:

Thanks for all the advice. I do have a strong faith, and an active noggin, but I had a down day when I wrote that last letter.

And thanks for helping Mother out of a jam. Damn it all, but I am going to ignore your warning and I am saying categorically, I'll pay you back one day, maybe in some other way than financially.

Now, after all those thanks, a rebuke. You made me sound in your last letter like a no-good bum recidivist old lag. I've once been in trouble for an electoral offence which was very minor indeed. So there!

Now to answer your questions: No, I cannot be contacted by telephone. Mother's birthday is December the 25th. When's yours?

Do I need anything? you ask. Well, yes, but not anything you can help me with. Like a radio, sunshine, a better backhand at badminton, more letters from you (you can do something about that), but most of all, I want to SEE you. Not that I could ever forget what you look like, but you know what I mean.

All my love, Kenner

He didn't seem to experience any shortage of things to write about:

As I write this letter, I am looking out onto a lake where yesterday there were fields. It has been the worst summer this century here in the UK and last night I experienced the worst storm I can remember seeing in this country. It rained cats and dogs from 9 pm yesterday to 5:30 this morning, with much thunder and lightning. Result: flooding, ruined crops and a humidity level reminiscent of a sweaty gorilla's armpit.

By the time you receive this note, Mother will have been here. She wrote the other day that she had heard from you. She so values your letters.

As you will have gathered, this letter I am writing whilst just about keeping awake. I made 400 pizzas today, plus beef stew and dumplings and chicken pies. All before 10.30 in the morning. This afternoon—breaded hake or grilled liver. So I'm out on my feet!

Wherever you go next, remember that one person's prayers and best wishes go with you. Those of your Welsh brother.

Your ever loving Kenner

Dear Kenner:

I'm not supposed to be sitting here writing a letter. I'm supposed to be working. I've been itching to sit down and write to you these past few days, but they've been so hectic that I haven't had a chance.

I finally got all your letters that went to Mum's house and had to be forwarded. It makes me so happy to get letters from you, whether they are out of date or not or whether you have anything to tell me or not. Just words on a piece of paper chatting about anything or nothing are fine.

Your last letters talking about your work in the kitchen were very interesting. I read them over a few times and got great delight out of closing my eyes and imagining you scooting around the kitchen: organizing here, doing this, that and the other thing, now tasting something, all with your white apron on and one of those delightful chef's hats. Now, of course, I don't know if you wear a chef's hat, but it was fun imagining that you do.

My four-month contract in Halifax had come to an end and I was off to look for more work. Eventually I ended up in Windsor, Ontario. Wherever I was, the letters kept coming and I always looked forward to seeing one waiting for me in the mailbox.

"Despite my better judgement," he wrote one time, "I will obey your requests and tell you something more of myself. I am loath to do so for I am a far less interesting person than you, and anyway, you already know most of it."

Although professing reluctance, he then presented a detailed curriculum vitae starting with his birth on May 12, 1950, as "the only child of Mrs. Primrose Elias Jones, retired nurse, aged 68, and the late John Elias Jones, senior civil servant, who died of TB in February of 1951, aged 27." He went on to say he had dark brown hair (with signs of thinning), a beard (with the odd grey hair) and was of slim build (though not for long unless he got some more exercise).

There followed a list of qualifications: "1968, A Level History, Geography, Scripture, Law and Politics, Syr Huw Owen Grammar School; 1968–71, BSc Economics (Hons), Sheffield University; 1970–71, Rhodes Scholar at University of Berkeley; 1972, Dip. Ed., Avery Hill College; 1978, External MSc, London School of Economics; now external student for PhD (Export Law), Henley College."

He said he was a "member of the Institute of Export Licentiate of the Association of Political Agents, an associate member of the Royal Schools of Church Music, Hon. Vice-President of the Welsh League of Young Liberals and Vice-Chairman of the Liverpool Liberal Association."

The list of special positions he had occupied in the past was a long and impressive one: "Crucifer to HRH The Prince of Wales, Hon. President of the Caernarfon Youth Council, Chairman of the Caernarfon Investiture Committee, Executive and Council Member of the Welsh Liberal Party; President of the London Union of Education Students, Reader in Comparative Constitutions at Henley College and Vice-Chairman (Organization) of the European Union of Liberal Democrats."

There was more. Kenner was also, he told me, a "member of the Court of the National Eisteddfod and an ordained and licensed preacher and reader in the Church in Wales." His fondness for music had secured him the position of "organizer of the Gwynedd County Youth Choir in 1966–70 and a place in the Welsh National Youth Orchestra playing second horn from 1968 to 1970."

His numerous local and national political posts

included "assistant to the Liberal Chief Whip from 1972 to 1974" and "co-drafter of legislation for the Referendum on the European Economic Community." In 1974 the National Assembly of Wales rated him the "most outstanding political agent of the year."

His pastimes included skiing—he had won a bronze medal in the slalom at the 1973 Lowlands Championship, he said—badminton and cooking. And he was a certified mountain climbing and walking leader.

As a student he had worked as a wine waiter, youth leader and an aide to a veterinary surgeon. His professional career started with employment as an area organizer for the Liberal Party from 1972 to 1979, coupled with being a peripatetic agent and campaign organizer for the European Liberal Democrats. For some years he gave interviews as the Welsh Liberal Party's economic and constitutional spokesman, wrote political broadcast scripts, as well as edited and produced national broadcasts.

This was followed by his job as a tourist assistant in Llandudno. That only lasted seven months before he moved on to become a special project analyst for British Leyland and export liaison executive with British Airways. Four months into that and he was arrested and sent to prison.

The curriculum vitae did not end there. Kenner gave me a brief rundown on his love life, starting with, at the age of five, his love for a girl who had the best crayons in class. After the usual teenage flirtations, he became engaged at the age of twenty-two to a drama student, with whom he lived for nearly three years. He ended by asking me to send my love because "that's what I need most."

It would be fair to say my denial-of-reality self-programming was operating smoothly. Anyone with basic mathematics only needed to look at the list of accomplishments he touted to realize that he would need to be decades older than he was to have completed all he claimed for himself at thirty. No, I didn't even bother to do some easy calculations. I just sat back, impressed. In fact, each time I opened a letter from Kenner, I found my heart racing, and I would skip to the last page and see how he signed it. Were his closing words, written in that bold turquoise ink, an attempt to hint at something more that friendship? "All my love, Kenner" didn't seem like the way one friend would write to another. So I dared to echo his words and began to sign "Love, Donna."

Oh, I could always say that I intended nothing more than friendship. But I knew better then, and I know better now as, decades later, I reread my own words. I was dropping a baited hook in the water, wondering, hoping to make a catch. I was afraid to try, and afraid not to. I wanted someone in my life who was fun, intelligent, different. How exciting if the person was from another culture. How wonderful if this person saw a boring, insignificant Canadian—which is how I saw myself—as someone special. The thoughts whispered to me and tempted me. And so my heartbeats would pick up speed whenever I went to my mailbox. And every letter showed me exactly the person I wanted to see.

The next time he wrote, Kenner explained that he had only two true friends, his mother and me, and he was glad that, thanks to me, his mother had been able to reach level ground financially. He said he was looking forward to being released on parole, that he'd had the first of five job interviews and that his employment prospects were looking positive. Even so, he was hard on himself:

This is a terrible letter because, although I am not feeling down, I am drawn to write you a sombre one, not funny, silly or weird as usual. How I wish I could look after Mother and you, but I am no good to man or beast locked in here. I am a failure. I am not there when my friends need me.

This was difficult for me to read. I felt I could see into his feelings, and there was not much, if anything, I could do to help other than continue to be encouraging, which I was in my next letter. But that single sentence about wanting to look after me stuck in my thoughts for a long, long time. I allowed myself to dream about what it would be like to have someone who wanted to take care of me. It opened a whole new landscape of daydreams. I wouldn't have to work. All needs would be met. I would have a provider and a champion. I could simply dedicate myself to living a loving and happy life. I had longed for that since I was a little girl.

"Your letters mean a great deal to me, you know," he replied:

I don't get regular visits and if a week goes by without a letter from the New World, I feel quite down. I can't explain it logically. It is just that knowing you have gone to the effort, amid all the other priorities of your busy round, to write to me. Well, it gets me quite choked at times.

You cannot imagine just how much one loses in coming into prison. Limited mail, no phone, selective censorship, limited freedom of movement, constant suspicion, early nights and no days off. I could go on.

But there has been one spin-off. This has been so very important that I think I'd go through it all again for the sake of it—I have felt a closer affinity to you.

Result: many sham friends, 18 months, a job, respect, prospects and self-incentive all lost. But a great friend gained.

Next time around, Kenner was in a more ebullient mood. "This week has been just about the best in ages and ages," he wrote, saying that he had received four letters from me in eight days and that he had a photo of me I had sent him. He had it pinned up in his prison cell next to postcards from Wales, the Lake District and the Rockies. He wanted to know how I was getting on with trying to learn the Welsh language, and wrote out the words to a Welsh hymn, *Calon Lân*.

When I had stayed with Primrose and him in Caernarfon, I had heard the beauty in the Welsh language, and been inspired to try to learn. Ruby had bought me a children's book to help me with basic words. She had laughed herself into a state of tears and gasped for breath over my attempts at pronunciation. That only encouraged me to read more and fuel her laughter. Those were highlight moments of fun. When I came home, I borrowed what books on the Welsh

language I could find from the library and ordered a Welsh–
English dictionary. Kenner was most supportive. The hymn
was presented as a challenge to see if I could translate it.

> *Nid wy'n gofyn bywyd moethus,*
> *Aur y byd na'i berlau mân:*
> *Gofyn wyf am galon hapus,*
> *Calon onest, calon lân.*
> *Calon lân yn llawn daioni,*
> *Tecach yw na'r lili dlos:*
> *Dim ond calon lân all ganu*
> *Canu'r dydd a chanu'r nos.*

I held my breath as I worked on the translation, searching through my dictionary, word by word:

> I don't ask for a luxurious life,
> the world's gold or its fine pearls,
> I ask for a happy heart,
> An honest heart, a pure heart.
> A pure heart full of goodness
> Is fairer than the pretty lily,
> None but a pure heart can sing,
> Sing in the day and sing in the night.

It was delightful, beautiful, deep. But was it just a hymn,
or a message? I chose to see it as being sent from the heart.
Romantic. To return the language challenge, I sent him one
of my favourite poems in French, a poem I had learned in
school: *La neige tombe*—"The Snow Falls"—by Jean Richepin.
I waited for him to respond. He never mentioned it. I was

reluctant to challenge him about ignoring my gift in return. I might be seen as nagging or competitive, and who would want to cultivate a relationship with a demanding, difficult person? Although I didn't say that to myself in that way, I know now it's what was in the back of my mind. So the beauty of my poetic offering melted away.

La neige tombe
Toute blanche dans la nuit brune,
La neige tombe en voletant.
O pâquerettes! Une à une
Toutes blanches dans la nuit brune.
Qui donc là-haute plume la lune?
O frais duvet! Flocons flottants!
Toute blanches dans la nuit brune
La neige tombe en voletant.

My translation was not expert:

The Snow Falls
All white in the brown night,
The snow falls and tumbles.
O daisies! One by one,
All white in the brown night.
Who up there peels the feathers of the moon?
O fresh down! Flakes floating!
All white in the brown night,
The snow falls and tumbles.

With the approach of his first winter in Her Majesty's Prison Ashwell, Kenner wrote about two commemorations that take place every November in the UK—Guy Fawkes Night and Remembrance Sunday—and about his "fervent" belief in the power of prayer: "I pray for you every day, and for myself, that I may be worthy of your friendship and of Mother's love."

The letters continued all through the fall and winter of 1980–81, and as I learned more and more about this Welsh friend of mine, I increasingly saw him as the kind of person I had always been looking for: someone with a sense of humour, kindness and courage to keep as cheerful as possible under extremely trying circumstances.

As the new year came around, Kenner wrote that he might be paroled in the spring:

> *Just think! I could be out of here in 10 weeks! Boy am I bored. It's so damnably tedious in here I could SCREAM. By the way, if you don't cart your body over here by the fall, I'll work 22-and-a-quarter-hour days to jet over there to tell you off. You hear me? I can't wait to see you.*

His next letter explained that

> *because of my postgraduate degree from the University of London, I have been sent a ballot paper this week for the election of a new vice-chancellor. The retiring holder is Her Majesty, the Queen Mother, who has held the position since 1955. The post is ceremonial, but with the practical responsibility as final arbiter of senate disputes.*
>
> *The nominees are: HRH The Princess Anne, Nelson Mandela and Jack Jones (a retired union*

leader). As the job requires 6–8 visits each year to constituent colleges (London School of Economics, Imperial College, etc.) and presence at award conferments, I feel that to elect an imprisoned man (regardless of the abhorrence I feel towards his captors) is irresponsible. Equally, to elect a man with no academic qualifications and with no sense of ceremony would be wrong. The result is I shall reluctantly vote for Anne. She is too young and not eminently suitable, but she is the least poor of the alternatives. Sounds like Carter and Reagan all over again.

I remember having a tumble of thoughts in my head as I read this. The first was that he truly moved in high circles. That thought was quickly followed by a tinge of skepticism. The skepticism was overruled by the idea that I didn't know enough about the culture in Britain to judge if he was telling me the truth or not. It seemed absurd. But the thought that won over all the rest was why would he bother to lie about something like that? People who cared about other people just didn't do that sort of thing. Or so I believed. I brushed aside—again—most of my doubts. One lingered like a stone in my shoe, but I chose to ignore it and walk on.

In the next few weeks, Kenner wrote that he would be getting a four-day parole in February to attend job interviews and would be home for good on March 16. It was, of course, a tremendous relief for him to have a final release date. It was something for me to look forward to, as well. I marked it on my calendar at work.

He had become very important to me. I was still too young and too unaware to know what was driving me straight into Kenner's web. It's easier to look back and see it now, though. I had been married before, and although the relationship ended as amicably as possible, I was left feeling unloved and unlovable. Who would want the frumpy, ordinary, unremarkable person I saw myself to be? And time was speeding by. My thirtieth year was on the horizon. No one had expressed any serious interest in me lately. That is, until Kenner appeared.

CONGRATULATIONS! The news of the finalization of your parole is great! Kenner, I truly believe every word when you say that you will make a place for yourself and re-establish yourself when you get out. Yes, I know it won't be easy to start from the bottom again. I know how that feels, too. But you are an intelligent person with a lot going for you.

If my letters to you have been of any comfort, that is wonderful. But know that I would have been a much less happy person this year if not for your letters. Just knowing somebody really cares, that somebody wants to know how I am doing, is a wonderful thing. And for months you have given that to me.

I marked my calendar with two important dates circled in red: the beginning of his four days of temporary parole; and March 16, the day of freedom.

Next week I shall be writing my letters to you on a train en route to Wales! Then back here for just two weeks.

This is proving to be a very difficult letter to write. You see, I want to talk to you from a position of freedom. I won't want to say anything different. It's just that I, oh, I don't know.

You said in a recent letter how much my letters have helped you settle into a strange environment. How much more so for me. But there is soon to be another change in my position. Your letters MUST NOT dry up then. I want us to continue correspondence. You see, you have become someone very, very special to me, my dear friend. I cannot express it better than that. I have always found it difficult to make more than very superficial friendships. Perhaps only once ever before you came into my life have I felt a friendship, a kinship, more vital and alive than my relationships with my family. Now you ARE family, and Oh God, I cannot wait to see you.

There, that's out of my system. It had to be said because I believe that the heart must not be silenced.

That's enough for one day. I'll write more in a day or so.

All my love, Kenner

I read this letter over a few times, just to make sure that it said what I thought it said. There was the hint of something more than a friendship. I felt excited and afraid at the same time. And yet a voice inside whispered that I still knew so little about this man. Dismissing the doubts as those of a timid person, I ignored that voice—as usual. Instead I waited with Kenner and counted the days until his temporary parole, knowing his plans for the first day. He would return to Caernarfon and make a phone call to Canada. I dared not leave my post by the telephone for even a minute, and before long the phone rang. My heart was pounding so hard I could hear it rattling my eardrums.

"Hello?" It was Kenner.

I don't recall much of the conversation—being such a long distance one, it was brief because neither he nor Primrose had much money to pay for a lengthy international call—but I remember not knowing what to say and simply enjoying hearing his voice.

The letters continued:

> I was so excited having the opportunity of speaking with you this week that I actually became nervous. Me! Nervous!! Look what an effect you have on me. I also found it impossible to express over the phone just what I felt in my heart. It didn't help having the neighbours and Mother all listening to the conversation. What I wanted to say, only in a more positive way, was Thanks for being there.

Thanks for walking into my little tourist hut in 1979. Thanks for keeping me sane by writing to me. Thanks for showing me that you care, and most of all, Thanks for being you.

Now if I ever feel low or am tempted to throw in the towel and live on my past accomplishments, I just think of you and become determined to start all over and succeed again. I owe you that. I owe it to myself, and to Mother, but most of all, I owe it to you. Now, when I wake up feeling defeatist, I just think of you, remember how lucky I really am, and really believe that, thanks to you, today is the first day of the rest of my life.

That line, so clichéd now, was fresher then. It thrilled me to think I might have a place in this person's future.

When I took this letter form out of my bag, I did not intend to write such a sentimental letter. A psycho-analyst once told me years ago that I was too cold, logical and analytical in my approach to life. I never allow my heart to rule my mind. I did once. I lived with a girl and we were engaged to be married, but we parted. And I vowed, 'Never again'. I am better off leaving sentiment and close relationships to people better able to cope with it. I still care for people, but never, for six years, as persons.

You have broken this resolve of mine to be a man of the mind rather than of the heart. Do you think you can cope with that idea?

Boy, what a heavy letter. But I had to let it all out just once.

Love you, Kenner

I remember putting his letter down and walking over to the window. I looked out over the rooftops and beyond. Yes. I had to admit to myself that I had fallen in love with him. I went back and soaked up the last line one more time.

The last letter from prison arrived. I read it over and over and I felt wonderful:

I have never felt so relieved. This dark episode in my life is over. It is you who has kept me going in here, you know. Oh, I know that I have a certain resilience and that I never would I have allowed myself to be beaten down under the 'machine' in here. Nevertheless, it is your company, your presence, your love, which have kept me above the general mass of prison automatons. Yes, I do mean automatons. Most in here, both warders and inmates, act like unthinking, uncaring clockwork zombies. Wake up, eat, work as little as possible, eat, work again under orders, eat, sleep, work again.

NOT ME! NEVER! I will not be subjugated to the 'norm'. I am ME—rough edges, foolishness and so, my love, like me for what I am.

I could write all day today, but I have no more paper. So will you accept a few words, but a lot of love? You will? Great!

Love, Kenner

The next letter that came was simply an entire sheet of paper with "I'M FREE!" written in huge, multicoloured letters.

CHAPTER 3

On Bended Knee

T he next few letters I received from Kenner were all about finding work.

> *Home at last after my travels in search of modus laborus. And joy of joys two letters from you waiting to greet me! So I just had to sit down and write to you this afternoon. I am ashamed not to have written for over a week. However, this past week I have travelled over 1,500 miles and on British roads that is a devil of a long way.*

I was very much interested in what he had to say about finding employment. After all, if there was something in the future for us and we had a family, he had to be able to support us. So the logical first step was to get a job. I was holding my breath, hoping to read the words that would support my hopes and dreams:

*In London on Wednesday I had three interviews
and then on to Exeter on Thursday and Barnstaple
on Friday. One job is with the Daily Star, a
national newspaper with the Express Group. The
paper is a tabloid with a 1.4 million run and I
have been shortlisted from among 110 applicants
for a marketing job. I have played on my contacts
with the press. You know most of it.*

As part of his working past, Kenner explained that when
he had worked for the Liberal Democrats, he had connected
with a printing company that created material for the political parties, and for businesses and travel agents. According to
Kenner, his work didn't take up all his time. So instead of
being idle, he connected with the printing business and helped
develop a travel magazine and a sales team to promote it. Far-
fetched? It certainly seems that way now. At the time it was
just another in a long string of amazing accomplishments
that he boldly claimed as his own. I was not the only one who
believed him and was impressed. He proudly reported that
the *Daily Star* called him for a second interview, attracted by
his published articles and press contacts. And there was more
good news:

*I have also been called for a second interview as
conference and tours organizer for the Chartered
Institution of Electrical Engineers. Both of these
jobs are in London.*
*The third job for which I have now been short-
listed is as assistant manager of a hotel on Exmoor.*

I enclose a brochure about it. After all, you'll be my guest there if I get the job.

Love and a transcendental hug, Kenner

Then at last: "Yippee! Hooray! I've got a job!"

My heart soared as I imagined how proud and relieved he must be. After all the time in prison, wondering if there was any kind of a future, any success for him in the world, he had found work.

Kenner was to be a Local Centres Officer at what was then called the Institution of Electrical Engineers, an esteemed organization offering engineering professionals a way to collaborate, keep on top of changing science and technology, and mentor new engineers entering their specialty.

Kenner would be involved in organizing and coordinating various branches of the institution in various parts of the UK. He would also promote the institution's connection with schools and conferences. It sounded complex and challenging—perfect for Kenner.

The pay in Canadian terms, he said, would be $15,000 a year, plus a car, expenses, a British Rail Pass and overtime pay after thirty-five hours.

I just cannot express how glad I am! I had to be in work by the end of June so that I can properly look after you when you come to visit.

Till soon then, all my love, Kenner

I felt so happy. At last he was being rewarded for his persistence in the face of misfortune.

The letters that followed made me happy, too, and by now I had recruited a friend to share my growing excitement. I worked with John, a kind and peaceful man who had done research with me on some documentaries at the television station. He had become like a brother. Each time a letter arrived I would phone to tell him I was on the way. When I arrived at his house, tea would be ready. We'd sit at the kitchen table; he'd fold his hands in front of him and say, "Okay, tell me." I would read him the letter, waiting for his reaction, hoping it would be what I wanted: confirmation that I was being told I was loved. John would always assure me that love really was there.

I would walk back home afloat in emotion. Yes, I was in love. Kenner had not been physically attractive to me, and that didn't matter. That wasn't what I was looking for. I was in love with the inner man.

I was planning to visit Britain in June. I suggested this to Kenner shortly after he was released from prison. He enthusiastically supported the idea. It would have been two years since I had met him in the tourist hut in Llandudno. So many things had happened in both our lives.

I would meet Kenner in London and spend a week or so there and then travel by train through mid-Wales to Caernarfon to see Primrose.

On a calendar on my desk at work I circled in bright yellow the date of my flight to Britain. As each day passed, I crossed it off with a huge black X.

As I arrived at the airport in Toronto, my heart was pounding. How was I going to last the next eight or so hours of flight time just sitting and looking at my watch every fifteen minutes?

There was no way out of it, though. Once the aircraft was off the ground I was a prisoner of time and air travel, left to my thoughts. I had brought a book to help me pass the hours. I didn't finish even one chapter. My eyes would rest on the words, but my mind was racing with excitement. I even caught myself turning pages automatically— then realizing I hadn't absorbed a single sentence. My journey was seemingly endless.

When we touched down at Heathrow Airport, outside of London, the excitement I had been trying to suppress came welling up. I felt myself starting to perspire. If only all those people standing ahead of me, waiting to get out of the aircraft, would just hustle along, I could be out and into the terminal.

Once through passport control I would collect my luggage and go through customs before getting to the arrivals lounge. That was where Kenner would be, of course, watching the monitor to see that my flight had landed and waiting by the exit door along with hundreds of others, hope flashing over their faces every time the doors opened that maybe this time the person they were waiting for would emerge.

Several jumbo jets had landed one after the other and I was in a swarm of fellow travellers. We were all trying to funnel ourselves through several passport checkpoints. I was in a line of at least fifty. There were a dozen lines just like the one I was in. We inched forward one by one, passports in hand.

As my line slowly diminished, I counted the people ahead of me. Twenty. Fifteen. Ten. And then, horror of horrors, the officer at the desk put a chain across our path and went off shift. Those of us in line had to disperse to the *ends* of other lines, which were equally as long as when we had begun more than an hour before.

I couldn't believe it. It seemed too cruel. Here I was stuck in line at passport control when really I just wanted to rush through and see Kenner.

But would he really be there waiting? What would he look like? Was I going to discover that my dreams and thoughts of love were just fantasies? Was I headed for adventure or disappointment? And when, oh when, would it be my turn at the passport desk?

After nearly two hours I finally cleared passport control, and went to the luggage carousel. It was as if the gods of travel were against me: my luggage was nowhere to be seen.

By now I was worried. Perhaps Kenner had come but hadn't waited for me. Maybe he thought I had missed the flight or for some reason I had decided not to come.

Through customs now, and lines that seemed to take forever again. But at long last, I was through everything and headed for the exit to the arrivals lounge. I stopped briefly, took a deep breath, smoothed my hair with my hand and walked through the doorway.

A panorama of faces stared at me. Where was he? How would I ever find him in such a crowd? I walked slowly, trying to look everywhere at once. Suddenly there he was, in the front of the crowd. He appeared shorter than I remembered, and his beard had grown in. His hair was longer and curlier than when I had seen him last.

He smiled and waved, and signalled me to walk to the left.

I felt relief that he was there. I was travel worn and tired, but I smiled in spite of it all. It took a moment or two before we came together. It was a warm but awkward moment or two. I felt so close to Kenner although we hadn't seen each other in years; he felt so familiar. Strangely, the only greeting that seemed proper at the moment was a handshake.

"I was worried you weren't coming after all," he said. "It took so long for you to get through. What happened? Oh, never mind that now. It's so good to see you. You look wonderful. Better than I remembered. But you must be tired. Would you like a cup of tea?"

He took my bag and we walked to a cafeteria at one end of the hall.

I recounted my bad luck in passport control and then at the baggage carousel. We talked about everything and nothing over a quick cup of tea before deciding that the best course of action would be to report my lost suitcase and then travel to London to check me into the hotel I had booked. Once that was finished, we would go for lunch.

After filing a luggage report, we made our way to the Underground. As we rambled along, I started to unwind a bit. It was so nice and so strange at the same time to be there with him. I knew from his letters that he had been just as excited and impatient for this reunion as I was. We were both covering our feelings with decorum.

At the hotel I checked in and put my carry-on case in my room. It was a dingy place, but it was all I could afford. There had been no question, no suggestion of my staying with Kenner. As a strict and dedicated man of religion— as he described himself—everything would have to be appropriate and proper ... old-fashioned, perhaps. That suited me.

And besides, until he said what he had to say, if any-thing, all I had was words on paper. I suspected we were both holding our cards close.

Kenner suggested we head for Selfridges, a major department store on Oxford Street. All this time our con-versation had been quite amiable and not directed to anything in particular. I asked him about his work and the place where he was staying in the town of Walton-on-Thames, outside of London. He had rented a room in a house and been travelling about twenty-five minutes by train each day to work. He explained that being out in the countryside gave him a break from the city. He prom-ised to take me out there in the next day or so to see for myself.

We arrived at the cafeteria. Once we had a tray of sandwiches and tea in hand, Kenner suggested we sit in a semi-circular booth. I tucked myself in and arranged my lunch in front of me.

Soon after we sat down, Kenner said, "You are going to have to tell me something, you know."

"What's that?" I asked.

I thought he was about to launch into a discussion on Canadian politics or my travel arrangements, or who knows what. He looked at me for a moment then down at his food and back up at me again.

"You will have to tell me when it is all right for me to ask you to marry me."

My cup stopped midway to my lips. A burning, prickling feeling began in the pit of my stomach and quickly spread right to the tips of my fingers.

I didn't know how to respond. My brain was whirling with a dozen different things all in the same moment. This man was asking me about marriage and we had not yet even held hands.

Kenner continued to sit there. Looking calmly at me. I had to say something.

"I . . . I . . . this is, well, this has come up so suddenly it's—"

He interrupted gently. "I know it has, but I simply could not wait any longer to ask you. You must think about it and let me know when it is all right for me to ask you formally. Oh, I realize I seem to be rushing things, but this is something I am very sure of. Well, come on, girl, finish your tea."

I still had my cup in mid-air. All thoughts of how thirsty and hungry I was had vanished. So, there it was, out in the open. And the next three weeks of my visit were still ahead of me. I wondered if Primrose knew about his plans. I wondered why I didn't say yes right away. I couldn't, though. I carried on eating my meal with a bright red face and a confusion of thoughts and emotions.

Eventually Kenner laughed. "Well, I see I have finally stumped you. Nothing to say?" He reached over and patted my hand, winked at me. "Never mind. I'll give you a chance to recover."

In the early evening he took me back to my hotel. I was exhausted. We arranged for me to meet him the next day at Savoy Place after he got off work. During the day, I would go back to Heathrow to collect my luggage—if indeed it had been found—and pass the rest of the day by myself until late afternoon.

As we parted in the hotel lobby, he lightly kissed me on the cheek, and turned to wave just before he went out of sight. Strange, perhaps, to have such a prim-and-proper parting. After all, the man had just proposed to me. But I told myself this was simply in line with his character and convictions. And besides, I was too tired to try to think anything through.

I went into my room and tried to sleep. Although I was depleted from all the travel, my thoughts were spinning. Marriage? Maybe life in Britain! Children? What was I going to say to him? When would I know it was time to tell him I would entertain his proposal? Still turning over my thoughts, I drifted into a deep sleep.

Next morning, I returned to Heathrow Airport. At the lost luggage counter they handed over my suitcase. By the afternoon I was refreshed, and after lunch at a café near the hotel I consulted my map again to decide my route to

Savoy Place, where I was to meet Kenner after work. I was staying very near Paddington Station, just to the north of Hyde Park. By walking to Paddington I could get to the Underground, where any one of three lines would eventually take me to a station called Embankment.

I decided to take the Bakerloo, one of the oldest lines in the London Underground system. The rumbling old coaches were finished with dark wood and deep red upholstery. Before long I was back in the sunshine with half an hour to spare before Kenner came out from work. I sat in the Victoria Embankment Gardens, close to the Savoy Hotel and the headquarters of the Institution of Electrical Engineers. I was still feeling a bit overwhelmed.

For me, this was one of the most beautiful parts of London. I had been there before, briefly as a tourist, but now I felt as though I almost belonged. Everywhere I looked it seemed there were things that had a bearing on my thoughts. Children were playing in a grassy section of the gardens. Would Kenner and I have children? And the news agent's stall was positioned near the entrance to the gardens. What papers would I read if I was living here? Every thought and question caused a little jolt to my system. So much to think about, so many ideas and plans.

Lost in my own world, I sat quietly there, but as the time neared five o'clock, I walked over to Savoy Place. Kenner came out the door and down the steps. He chatted momentarily with someone and then walked over to where I stood. Watching him come toward me, I again took in his appearance. He was short, always surprisingly short to me from a distance. As he got closer, I could see his eyes and his smile. I smiled in return.

"Hi! How was your day?" I asked.

It seemed so easy, so natural to be there waiting for him. We went for dinner at a café and then passed the evening walking around the area. He held my hand, or tucked my arm into his, keeping his free hand on top of mine. I felt cherished. Kenner knew a lot history of London and kept up a commentary as we went along.

He saw me home to my hotel, gave me a brief kiss good-night and left for Waterloo Station to take the train to Walton-on-Thames.

The plan for the next day was for me to meet him after work, go with him to Waterloo Station and on to Walton-on-Thames, where he would have a reservation at an Italian restaurant. After dinner he would show me around the town before I took a late train back to London.

We met as arranged and headed for Waterloo Station. It was cavernous, noisy. Train schedules changed on huge boards hanging in the hall. The letters and numbers were constantly updated by a flutter of rotating cards that sounded like a flock of birds flying by at close range and high speed. An almost unintelligible voice boomed over the loudspeaker system, echoing off the walls. People were hurrying in every direction, seemingly knowing where they were going. Trains arriving and departing. Shops and stalls everywhere, and above the pandemonium a wide, lofty ceiling.

Soon we were on board our train and on our way out of London. The dingy brick and plaster backyards eventually gave way to more open spaces as we rolled west into Surrey.

The train stopped at stations en route: Esher, Hersham. And then we were at Walton-on-Thames. We left the station and walked into the town along quiet streets shaded by overhanging trees. Gardens threatened to overwhelm some of the homes they surrounded. Everything was clean and lush. The smells of summer filled the air. I could not resist thinking about what it would be like to live there. I found it so appealing and felt completely charmed.

The Italian restaurant was right beside the Thames. It was an intimate, romantic place, with thick plaster on the walls and an attentive host. The lights were low. Candles and flowers dressed the few tables. We drank wine and laughed and talked. The time passed quickly. With only an hour until the last train to London, we left the restaurant to walk back to the station.

Dusk had fallen and we strolled through the fading light. After a few minutes of walking in silence, Kenner said, "You really are very cruel, you know."

"What? What do you mean?"

What had I done? I didn't know.

"You have been keeping me waiting for an answer."

He stopped and turned me to face him.

"But Kenner, it's early yet. I need time to think."

That wasn't true. In fact I had been thinking, but now I hesitated, unsure what to say or how to say it.

"I cannot wait for you to think any more. You know who I am and you know how I feel about you. You must give me an answer now."

"But . . ."

My heart was pounding, and two different sides of my brain were shouting at me: Tell him yes; you know how you feel—why wait? No, don't rush into anything; you have time to think some more—take that time. Tell him yes . . . make him wait.

Kenner wasn't going to wait. He got down on one knee right there on the street, with cars and people going by. He took my hand and said, "Don, will you marry me? I am going to stay right here until you say yes."

I just had to laugh. He looked so sincere and so ridiculous at the same time.

"Kenner, get up!"

"Not until you say yes!"

"Kenner, get up! People are looking at you!"

"Let them look. I don't care. Tell me now—yes or no?"

I stood there gazing down at him, my hand in both of his, listening to my brain argue with itself. And then I decided.

"Yes."

"What did you say?" He almost shrieked the words.

"I said *yes*."

We looked at each other a moment longer. Then he stood up, put his arms around me, held me close and kissed me.

"You have made me the happiest man in the world. And I will make you happy. You'll see. You'll never want for anything and I will love you forever."

With our arms around each other we walked to the train.

CHAPTER 4

Wanting and Waiting

Overlooking Regent Street not far from Piccadilly Circus is London's oldest Indian restaurant, Veeraswamy. Winston Churchill, Indira Gandhi and Charlie Chaplin were among the many famous people said to have dined there since it opened in 1926. Kenner had made reservations and in we walked, hand in hand. I had never been in a place like this. The superb aromas of Indian cuisine swept down the stairs and through the open door. The first-floor room was lit with chandeliers and light from the tall windows. The elegant furniture, the lush carpets and the liveried waiters transported me.

I was eager to appear sophisticated enough to fit in, but I had no knowledge of Indian dishes. Indian cuisine was completely outside the realm of my experience. I tried to stay calm and on my toes.

A handsome maître d', elegantly and traditionally dressed, showed us to our table. I settled in and looked around. Was this fine restaurant an indication of the life ahead of me? Would I be treated to adventures that I hadn't even imagined? There was so much to experience, explore, learn.

After a short while we were invited to go to the buffet. I recognized none of the dishes, not even from the printed cards at the front of each tray. A waiter stood nearby, ready to serve. I was looking forward to tasting everything.

I placed a few spoonfuls of brightly coloured, aromatic, unknown foods on my plate and then arrived at something I thought I recognized but had never tasted.

"Oh—curry!"

"Yes, madam," said the man standing behind the trays. He was dressed in rich brocades and a turban. "It is the finest in London."

Kenner watched me with amusement as I tried to decide. The curries were labelled mild, medium and vindaloo.

"Vindaloo." Now, that sounded interesting. I was really intrigued. "I'd like to try that one."

"It's a hot one, Don," said Kenner. "I'm not sure you are up to it being that spicy."

The words were a challenge to my pride.

"I think I'd like to try it."

"Are you sure, madam?"

The waiter, looked at me. His eyes were gently saying, Don't do it. But I had charted my course.

"I would like to try some, please."

He smiled and served me.

I reached the end of the buffet with a loaded plate and we returned to our table. I began. The flavours were nothing short of awesome, blends of seasonings and spices that were new and wonderful. I worked my way around the plate, eventually arriving at the vindaloo.

It smelled superb. Mmm. I took a forkful and put it in my mouth— My world exploded. Oh my God! I needed every bit of self-control not to spew out whatever it was that had set my mouth on fire. I tasted nothing, had only the sensation of burning coals roaring up into my nasal passages, my eyes.

Meanwhile, the waiter had gone to the kitchen and was now standing just out of my line of sight, holding a glass of milk. He approached our table.

"Oh, so sorry, madam. So sorry. Here, quickly. Drink this."

I was obviously not the first guest to make the mistake of pitting myself against spices far beyond my capabilities.

The waiter handed me clean napkins and helped me mop the tears that streamed from my eyes. He did his best to make me comfortable.

"I should not have given you the vindaloo, madam. It is my fault entirely. I am truly sorry."

His heartfelt apologies were most kind. The milk had quenched the fire. My tears had stopped flowing. I collected myself and found I could smile at my silliness.

Eventually I could taste things again. The kind waiter made sure he wasn't too far away. I was in good hands.

My three weeks in Britain flew by in a blur of travel, planning and love. Kenner implied that in keeping with his Christian beliefs, there would be no intimate encounters until we were married. But that didn't mean there wasn't romance. While behaving like the perfect gentleman, he still managed to weave a spell around me. He would hold my hand firmly and let go only reluctantly. When he introduced me to people or carefully pulled my chair out to seat me at the table, he would do so with an elegance and air that signalled to the world that he considered me something special, someone irreplaceable.

His kisses were always in private, not long and lingering yet filled with feeling. He would put his hands on either side of my face and look me in the eyes. "I still can't believe it," he would say. Then we would both laugh. Yes, I was completely happy, and felt that even though my heart was full, the best was still to come.

Kenner took me to his favourite haunts in London. The city was all new to me now, filled with the fun of exploring hand in hand. And on my hand was an engagement ring. Kenner had presented it to me in his usual gallant style at a restaurant in Covent Garden. It was a lovely ruby, surrounded by tiny diamonds. It was easily the most beautiful ring I had ever seen.

We caught the train to North Wales to see Primrose and confirm what she already knew. Although my preference would have been to marry soon and begin our life together, Kenner wanted to wait a year. He felt it would make sense to set ourselves up with a better financial base than what we had at the moment. Reluctantly I agreed. I would return to Canada, save as much as possible for the down payment on a family home, and Kenner would do the same. I quelled my disappointment, persuading myself that being practical was a good idea.

Our days together vanished. I left Kenner and came

home, my heart carrying a strange combination of heaviness and happiness. A year, he assured me, would pass quickly.

It seemed somehow strange to find myself back in Canada. I had returned to my job at the CBC in Windsor, Ontario. I spent much time reflecting on the conversations Kenner and I had had about when to marry, where to live, how soon to start a family. It was so easy for me to imagine a house full of children. They would be a combination of Canada and Wales, the great outdoors and music, love and challenge.

I also pondered what kind of man Kenner was. He was a wonderful conversationalist. He was interested in the world. He seemed fearless, curious, dedicated. Yes, he was still that slightly scruffy little Welshman I had met in my summer of travel. But seeing him dressed in a good suit, full of confidence, I now found him very attractive. Yes, this was the man for me.

Kenner was a practising Anglican and appeared to be unapologetically dedicated to his faith. I, on the other hand, was more of a spiritual seeker. I'd attended the Pentecostal Church as a youngster, but it was too zealous for me as I came into my teens. I explored some Eastern philosophies and traditions, and considered myself an appreciator of any and all spiritual paths that focused on peace, love, healing and forgiveness. Kenner suggested that I become a baptized Anglican to create unity in our home. He explained that when we had children, he would like them to be brought into the church, and felt it would be easier for us all if he and I were in accord on the subject of faith. I was willing to consider it. I made an appointment at All Saints Anglican church in Windsor.

When I was shown into Canon Peck's office, he welcomed me with a warm smile and a handshake. He was a man of barely medium height and build. His gentle, open energy immediately put me at ease.

"So, tell me what I can do for you," he said.

He relaxed into his chair, folded his hands together over his knees and smiled encouragingly.

"Well . . ." I hesitated, searching for my words. "This may sound a bit odd, but I'm wondering about becoming an Anglican. The thing is, I don't really know anything much about the Anglican Church."

He didn't react as though it was a silly comment at all.

"Tell me why you're considering this."

I explained about Kenner, my upcoming marriage and our plans for a family.

"I think it would be a lot easier for me to become an Anglican than for him to become, well, less structured. So I thought I'd speak to you and see about it."

We chatted for a while about the path my spiritual life had taken, and when I got to the Eastern philosophies part, he perked right up.

"Your journey sounds very much like mine." He smiled. "I was raised in the Baptist Church, and when I became a young man, I went and studied at an ashram in India. But then I found my home in the Anglican Church and here I am."

That was encouraging. "But I don't really know anything about being an Anglican," I said. "Are there special studies, ceremonies? I mean, what kind of a version of

Christianity is it? What do you people believe? How would I know if I could be an Anglican?"

He considered a moment. "I think it's very simple. You've had some education about Jesus and the Bible?"

I nodded.

"So let me ask you this: In any situation, modern situation, right now, if Jesus walked through the door and into the room, can you imagine what he would do or what he would say?"

I thought about this. It seemed clear to me. "Yes. I could."

Canon Peck smiled. "Well, that's it. That's really what it's all about. Nothing more complicated. If you know that, you have all the understanding you need. Come to a service next Sunday and just see what you think, see if you feel comfortable, and then we'll talk again."

I did. I walked into the church the next Sunday and somewhat self-consciously sat in a pew near the back. The church was a beautiful, bright space, with light, warm wood. The music was gentle. Everyone was bustling and smiling.

When the service began, I stayed seated, not knowing the ceremonies or rituals. But it didn't seem to matter. Almost immediately I felt as though a thick, warm blanket had been wrapped around me. I sat quietly, surrounded by peace.

The following Sunday I was baptized. The Sunday after that I was confirmed. It felt good.

How strange to reflect back on that moment with the benefit of time and distance. While I was embracing in a formal way the principles of a Christian life, the man I was to marry was, for all his show of piety and commitment, only pretending. But that day in the church in Windsor it didn't even cross my mind that he was anything other than what he appeared to be.

As Kenner had assured me, the time did pass quickly—more quickly than I had expected. My reporting at CBC Windsor was all-absorbing and always a challenge. Chores and ordinary life on my own used up my days off. Nonetheless I crossed off with an X on my calendar every single day that went by.

In the solitude of my apartment I had plenty of time to think. During those final days before I left Windsor, I wrote to Kenner, expressing my feelings of love and doubt. Reading the letter many years later, I see a young woman daring to hope that the future would fulfill her dreams and that disappointment wasn't lurking around the corner:

> *It will be so nice to belong to someone and to have at least you as something stable in my life. You know, I have to stop and remember that it is all really very close—that I am not saying it's a matter of months until you and I are married, it is now simply a matter of weeks, days! I have to remind myself that I am making a commitment for life, and is this really what I want? Do I have second thoughts? Am I confident in my decision?*
>
> *I have thought it over many times. I have tested myself by toying with the idea that maybe this was just a passing thing, or maybe I just let you talk me into it, or maybe it was just an adventure that appealed to me, or maybe just a way to get out of*

Windsor, or maybe I really shouldn't do this because I would lose the background I have built in the CBC, maybe, maybe, maybe . . .

Every single time, every single time, I get the same answer—the most important thing in this world to me is you, and everything else takes a back seat. You are the right person for me. I love you and want to be with you and am anxious to start to build a life together. There is never any doubt after I ask myself those questions.

But I do have the feeling that I hope it is all happening the way I think it is, and that you really are in love with me, and that you really do want to marry me and share your life with me. But I won't know for sure until I step into the church and see you waiting there. Then I'll know it's not just a dream.

CHAPTER 5

The Wedding

My family lived in a farming area on Vancouver Island on Canada's west coast. I've always enjoyed telling people that I was raised in North Oyster. Yes, it is a real place. It is a district between the town of Ladysmith and the city of Nanaimo. In the 1950s and '60s shopping excursions in North Oyster were infrequent and limited in scope. But in those days travelling salesmen still roamed the rural communities with their sample cases and charming smiles. They often made a stop at our home on Cedar Road.

I remember the fun of watching the Fuller Brush man open his suitcase full of wares on the coffee table in our living room. He always had an audience of children pressing to see what was in there, the fascinating array of housekeeping supplies all tidy and tucked into place. Mum usually bought something.

Then there was the Watkins man, whose flavourings and spices were less interesting somehow. A few vacuum cleaner salesmen came by, but they were quickly and politely turned away.

The soft-spoken but confident Bernina Sewing Machine man was more persuasive. So was his machine. It was a beauty, and wonderfully engineered. It sewed every type of fabric he fed through. It purred while creating perfect stitches. Mum took a deep breath and said yes. I learned to sew on that Bernina. It was the early sixties and I put in many hours turning out trendy clothes in colours and styles that shocked our elders.

But those days had since passed and now I was living in a basement in Windsor, Ontario. I was still working at the CBC and making a fair wage, but I had given up my apartment in a heritage home and moved to a budget suite. The more money I could save, the more I could send to Kenner to build up our house fund in Britain. My furniture consisted of an air mattress, a folding card table, two folding chairs, an ironing board and a television. My clothes and personal items were arranged in cardboard boxes. I didn't mind because it was only temporary and a way for me to save and contribute to our future.

Kenner and I were to be married on Vancouver Island at an Anglican church called St. Philips-by-the-Sea, near Nanaimo. Father Martin, a kind, cheerful Dane, would preside.

I decided to make my wedding dress. But the Bernina was long gone and a new machine would be an unnecessary expense when I was trying so diligently to save.

Undeterred, I went down to a local fabric store and chose a dress pattern and some airy chiffon in a soft, ivory shade with matching satin. I brought everything home and set to work. I laid the fabric out on the floor and pinned the pattern on. Then I carefully cut out the dress and put each piece aside, ready to be stitched by hand.

Each evening when I was watching television or just sitting quietly, I would perch on the end of the air mattress with the dress draped over my lap. There was something soothing and satisfying about putting in every bit of thread deliberately, every stitch carefully. I thought about how happy I was and how much I was looking forward to the new chapter in my life. I also felt subtly connected to generations of women before me who had sat quietly and created clothing for themselves and others, sometimes for celebrations, sometimes just for survival. Once in a while I wished for the Bernina, but mostly I was content with my simple tools of a needle and a spool of thread.

When the final hem was complete, the zippers in, every last button and hook attached, I tried my wedding dress on. It was perfect.

As the date for the wedding approached, I resigned from my job, packed up the things in my basement apartment and filled two large suitcases with what now remained of my personal possessions. I folded the wedding dress carefully, and layered it with tissue paper to keep it from crushing.

Mum had set everything in motion for the wedding, scheduled for July 3. We all arrived close to the day. A flurry of trips to and from the airport brought me, and then a few days later Kenner and Primrose, to the island. The weather was sunny and warm, with only a few clouds carrying the possibility of a light summer shower.

Primrose had settled in and was delighting everyone with her feisty attitude and Welsh accent. She'd perch her sturdy self on a chair, her legs dangling, and sit there with her arms crossed as she observed everything going on. She was quick to join in conversations with a story or simply to laugh. Primrose charmed everyone she met, as did Kenner. Here was this smart, kind, fun-loving person who brought a bit of the wide world with him when he came in the door. Kenner wanted to know everything about the farm. He explored the barns and fields, walked around the cattle, sat on the dock and looked out at the lake. The place was paradise, he said.

On the day of the wedding, the sun was shining through a sprinkling of rain. All preparations had gone smoothly. The ceremony was to be in the early afternoon; then we'd all go back to the house for the reception. After the reception Kenner and I would head for Victoria, the capital of British Columbia, about an hour's drive to the south. We had arranged to spend the night at the stately Empress Hotel and then take a ferry to Seattle the next morning. From there we'd fly to Hawaii for our honeymoon.

But first, the ceremony. In keeping with tradition, I was the last to arrive at the tiny church. I took a deep breath, trying to calm myself, and walked up the few steps to the open door. My dress made a soft, swishing sound as I moved. I carried a bouquet of deep pink and magenta sweet william—Kenner had said it was his favourite flower. I had two roses tucked into the bouquet, almost out of sight.

The church was full, with every available seat taken. An expectant hush had settled over the congregation. As I entered the church, there was Kenner at the front, standing quietly, hands folded, smiling at me. I felt myself relax and I smiled back.

Even walking slowly, it took only seconds to arrive at the altar. I tried to look at everyone along the way. I was so overwhelmed with happiness it was easy to return smiles. At the altar I handed my bouquet to my sister and took Kenner's hand.

At the end of ceremony, I pulled the two roses from my bouquet and gave one to Kenner. I went to my mother and Kenner went to his. We handed each a rose. Their faces showed delight and surprise. Then we went to the signing table and, using Kenner's gold fountain pen, wrote our names in bold turquoise script. I was now Mrs. Kenner Elias Jones.

Out of the church and in the sunshine, we got into a car, to be driven back to the house. Kenner had put two gifts for me in the back seat and presented them as we settled in for the ride. One was a Welsh love spoon. The wooden spoons are a traditional gift from a groom to his bride. They were customarily carved by the husband-to-be. The number of hearts, circles or spheres carved into the handle were meant to indicate how many children he hoped the marriage would bring. The spoon Kenner gave me had three connected hearts.

The second gift was an Anglican Church Book of Common Prayer.

"We're going to be living a Christian life," he said. "I thought it was fitting that you have a copy of your own."

I smiled happily, the book, flowers and love spoon in my lap. The short drive gave us a chance to snuggle in the back of the car. I looked down at the ruby-and-diamond engagement ring and the wedding band now beside it. My world seemed new.

Before long the reception was under way. Guests trickled in to enjoy the abundant food and music and the mercifully short speeches. Kenner got up and spoke about how happy he was to now be part of this large Canadian family. He promised to take very good care of me.

When the celebrations over, we changed into travelling clothes, put the suitcases in the car and left for Victoria amid a shower of good wishes.

Wedding days are often described as a moment in a fairy tale—the gossamer dress; the flowers; procession; the smiling, adoring husband. I had soaked in every moment of my day. My eyes and ears were open, heart overflowing. There was nothing I would change, nothing left undone and unsaid. However, I had no idea then what kind of fairy tale I was actually in, and what kind of ending awaited me. The happy princess of the moment knew nothing except the gold and sparkle of the day.

At the Empress Hotel we were shown to our room. It was not a posh honeymoon suite by any means, but I couldn't have cared less. The next morning, we were off on the ferry to Seattle. It was a long day of travel, but as we pulled into the dock in Seattle, fireworks lit up the sky. It was the Fourth of July. We joked that the celebration was for our benefit.

I had never been to Hawaii and was thrilled when we arrived in Maui. We explored Lahaina, swam, slept on the sandy beaches, ate fabulous seafood each night surrounded by torchlight on a restaurant patio, made love in the fading light and slept in each morning.

We didn't talk much about the future, just some generalities. Kenner didn't seem to want to make plans. He said the house money I had been saving and sending was safe and waiting for us, and we'd take things one step at a time. I would find a job to supplement the family income. Eventually we'd buy our house and start our family. I felt impatient but was willing to take a deep breath and just let things unfold.

CHAPTER 6

My New Home

I was now living in England married to a British subject and so was eligible to apply for "the Right of Abode in the United Kingdom." For the first few weeks, we lived in a rented townhouse in Weybridge, Surrey. We'd go for walks along the Thames in the evening and just enjoy our surroundings and each other. There were swans on the water and a weir to explore. Everything was new and different. I wasn't working just yet and so spent my time settling in and establishing a routine.

It was summer, and the days were long and sunny. Kenner always seemed to wake up earlier than me. By the time I opened my eyes he had already breakfasted on toast and coffee and was back upstairs. I would lie in bed under a light, crisp cotton duvet and watch him getting ready for work.

"Good morning, sleepyhead." He'd smile at me, buttoning up his white shirt.

"Good morning. You're up early."

"I can't just lie around like some people." He'd laugh. "You Canadians seem to expect a luxurious lifestyle." He'd finish attaching his cufflinks and adjust the cuffs. His wallet was tucked into an inner pocket in his jacket along with his gold fountain pen. "Well, that's just fine." He'd smile again. "That's what I'll be giving you."

He'd sit on the edge of the bed, lean down and kiss me. "I'll see you at dinnertime, Don. You just enjoy yourself today."

Then he'd stand and look at me a long moment. "I still can't believe it," he'd say.

"What?"

"That you're here. That you're mine."

With a last smile and wave he'd be off. I'd wait until I heard the front door close and then I'd hop out of bed.

The conversations might vary slightly each morning, but inevitably, with Kenner's departure, so would begin another day of contentment. I was exploring my surroundings, learning about a different culture and reinventing myself.

After breakfast this particular morning I cracked open a recipe book and searched for inspiration. There were things I didn't feel confident in trying to prepare, such as rabbit or beef heart. That would have to wait until Kenner had a day off. He was a very good cook so I decided to leave some of the adventurous dishes until I saw him do them first. However, I had discovered that the British make superb sausages, so they were going to be on the dinner table tonight. That I could manage.

I headed for the shops. As I walked, I encountered other

women coming and going. I smiled and said, "Good morning." Occasionally one would smile and answer back. Each time I would think: I'm glad to see you are happy, but there is no way you could possibly be as happy as I am.

Into the butcher's, the baker's, the shop with the fruits and vegetables. Eventually my basket was full. The last stop was a florist shop. Dahlias were abundant and the flower bins were crowded with huge bundles of colour. I asked the price.

"Just a pound, luv," said the robust and smiling man.

I chose a brilliantly coloured bunch, paid for it and laid the flowers across the top of the purchases in my basket.

Our stay in Weybridge was temporary. Kenner suggested, and I agreed, that it would make sense to take a bit of time and see where we would like to buy a home. We found a place to rent in the village of Winchmore Hill near Amersham in Buckinghamshire. We moved to a small house on Fagnall Lane with the idea of living there for a year, exploring the surrounding communities and finding our forever home. Buckinghamshire was beautiful, with large areas of open countryside. It was also within comfortable commuting distance of London.

I was in line for a job at CBC Radio in London as an assistant to the producer of radio current affairs. But the position wasn't coming open for two more months. In the meantime, I tried out at a temp agency for secretarial staff.

After submitting my CV and having an interview, I was given a typing test. I was shown into a cramped, airless room with pale blue walls. There was a single desk and an Olivetti electric typewriter. The woman conducting the test gave me a sample document to type. I rolled a clean sheet of paper around the platen, settled myself as comfortably as I could and took a deep breath. It felt to me as though a lot was riding on this test. I needed to make money to contribute to our living expenses. To pass, I had to do at least sixty words a minute with minimal mistakes. Those were the days before word processing. Mistakes in typing meant lost time and wasted paper. It had been a long time since I'd had to demonstrate my skills.

I looked at her and nodded. She clicked the stopwatch. "Go." Off I went, fingers flying. I tried not to allow any doubts to creep in. Instead I thought of my high school typing teacher, Mrs. Frost. She was a tiny, willowy Englishwoman who had immigrated to Canada in her middle years. Mrs. Frost had fly-away white hair, knobby fingers and long, crooked teeth. She also had an energy level that was off the charts. Everything she did, she did quickly, and of course expected that from the rest of us. Her high-pitched voice cut easily through the clatter in a room filled with manual typewriters:

"All right, class. Clear your minds. Put your eyes on your copy. Relax your fingers. Take a *deep* breath, and— A A A B B B C C C . . ." She emphasized starting slowly with rhythm and gradually increasing speed.

When I heard the stopwatch click in the temp agency office, I set off at a measured pace then slowly picked up speed as my fingers became familiar with the Olivetti's keyboard. I shut out everything except the words on the page.

"Done. That's it. Thank you."

The woman conducting the test rolled the paper out of

the typewriter. "Just wait outside for a moment," she said. "I'll calculate your results."

A short time later she came through the door with a smile on her face. "Well done," she said. "Seventy-five words a minute and not a single mistake. You're hired."

Thank you, Mrs. Frost.

Kenner seemed both delighted with my success and relieved by it. He had been assuring me that our household finances were in good shape with the money he was bringing in; consequently I hadn't been worried. So I was a bit surprised to hear a tone of urgency in his voice as he asked when and how I would be paid and how much money I would be making. I felt a bit hurt, thinking that I had already sacrificed, worked hard and saved diligently to help us begin our lives together. But, as usual, I just swallowed my doubts and tried to be a willing and contributing partner. I headed for my first day as a temp.

The London agency sent me to work at a law firm in Lincoln's Inn Fields, a large public square surrounded by buildings steeped in time. Everything looked old, stately and serious. The stairs leading up to front doors of the law firm were so worn they dished in the middle. I felt as though I was walking into a Dickens novel.

Soon after introducing myself, I was escorted back out the door and over to a wrought-iron gate. Through the gate and down another set of uneven steps, I came into a basement workroom. This, I was told, was the typing pool. My desk was a small table with a huge manual typewriter. It was the 1980s and many of the documents prepared for court in Britain were still created on large pieces of heavy paper then adorned with ribbons and wax seals.

After being given my instructions, I set to work. It took both hands to roll the paper around the platen and into the correct position for typing. Before long the clacking of my keys joined the racket already in the room. I was one of six typists toiling away. The job was tedious, but not without moments of fun. The women with whom I worked were quiet and diligent—with the exception of Sue, an irrepressible cockney as wide as she was high who ruled the typing pool. Sue didn't let too much time go by without injecting her personality into the room.

"Hey!" she called out one morning. "Hey! Dorothy! Did I tell you what my guy is getting me for Christmas?"

"No," Dorothy replied. The tempo of the typewriter keys slowed considerably as we all paused to listen.

"Oh yes," said Sue. "Oh yes. I told him, I did. I told him it had bloody well better be a diamond in my Christmas stocking or he wasn't getting near any other of my stockings, mark my words." She let out a rolling, robust laugh and carried on, unconcerned. "Yes, he'd better be putting a diamond right here." She held out her left arm, spreading and waving her chubby fingers.

After lunch we were beginning again, when Sue swept in. "Sorry I'm late, ladies," she said. "But I had a devil of a time finding me tights for tonight. Ohhh, didn't I tell you my man is taking me for a fancy dinner? Oh yes!"

She pulled a package of pantyhose out of a shopping bag, ripped the top off the plastic and removed them. Then she put the toes of the pantyhose on the floor in front of her, stepped on them, trapping them firmly under her shoes, and grabbed the pantyhose by the waist. With great effort she hauled and stretched, hauled and stretched. We all just sat and stared, waiting for them to rip apart. Somehow they held together. Sue continued to pull with all her might.

"Well, what are you all looking at?" she said, laughing. "They never make them big enough for me. I've got to do this or I can't get me fat little legs into them." The room exploded with laughter, Sue's the loudest of all.

CHAPTER 7

Something Wrong

S oon it was summer then autumn, and the trees in our little Buckinghamshire village were turning to golds and browns. All along Fagnall Lane the air was filled with a soft, leafy smell. The nights were closing in. We had established a rhythm to our days of work, long walks and weekends.

I learned many things about my new husband. For example, he told me one day that he was a member of the Royal Naval Reserve. Kenner appeared to be quite proud of his commitment and patriotism. He explained that he had been serving in the RNR as much as possible in between various travels and contracts. Since our lives now had a pattern and predictability, he felt he could pick up his training and service again, and so he did.

Kenner would disappear every Wednesday evening for a few hours. He told me he was off to meet, train, learn, whatever was on the agenda that night in his reserve group. When he came home, he always had some information to share about what had gone on that night. It was very interesting and a part of life I knew nothing about. I didn't question; I just supported him. He didn't have a uniform at home. When I asked about that, he explained that the uniforms were kept in lockers at the barracks and only brought out for ceremonial purposes. I realize now that it didn't make sense. At the time I experienced zings of fear and doubt, but I didn't challenge him. Besides, I thought, I have no experience with anyone doing any sort of military service, so maybe what he's telling me is right. But a nagging feeling wouldn't vanish. It kept tapping me on the shoulder. It lodged in my gut and tried to make me pay attention. I found myself wondering if he was up to something. Was this explanation of military commitment just a cover for something else?

There was nothing in the house, in his personal possessions that linked him to time with the Royal Naval Reserve. There were no pictures, mementoes, schedules. Yet surely he wasn't lying to me. I would watch him when he came home, but he would easily describe the events of the evening. I stifled the doubts.

Just before Remembrance Sunday that year, Kenner arrived home from an evening with the reserve carrying a uniform. He told me he was required to wear it for the ceremony at the local war memorial. We planned to go to the parish church early on Sunday and then on to the memorial service in the nearby town of Beaconsfield.

The day before the service Kenner suddenly reported that he had sprained an ankle. He said didn't really know how this had happened, but he claimed that his ankle was very sore and that he couldn't put any weight on his foot.

I offered to wrap his ankle for him, but he didn't want that because he wouldn't be able to put his shoe on. Instead he opted to use a cane. I didn't remember us having such an item in the house, but he produced one out of a closet. He practised hobbling about and decided he would be able to navigate his way around adequately.

Sunday morning, we arrived at church. Kenner looked smart in his Royal Naval Reserve uniform. People noticed that he was struggling to walk, but he put on a brave face. After the service a number of parishioners came up to him to offer sympathy about the sprained ankle and to admire him in his dress blues. Then off we went to the war memorial.

For everyone there the Falklands War was still top of mind. It had begun in the South Atlantic in April when Argentina invaded and occupied the Falklands, a British territory. Britain wasn't sitting still for that and the conflict was under way. By the time it was over, 649 Argentine and 255 British military personnel had died, along with three Falkland Islanders. So it was no surprise that when Kenner arrived at the war memorial, he drew attention.

I tried to feel proud but instead was incredibly uncomfortable. Again and again I would cringe as people walked up to him to shake his hand and commiserate with him about his limp and his cane. They thanked him for his patriotic contribution. They assumed he had been injured in the Falklands conflict. He did nothing to set them straight.

As we drove home, I wanted to speak up. I wanted to challenge him. Why had he let everyone believe he was a war veteran? Why did he offer a smile of quiet courage to those who expressed concern? Why was his ankle suddenly much better when we got home? This was a perfect opportunity for me to confront myself, too. Why was I refusing to face what was right in front of me? The only answer I can give to myself now, so many years later, is that deep down I knew the answer. Somewhere in my heart and in my mind a part of me did recognize the imposter. I simply didn't have the skills or confidence to face it. And I was too afraid.

Kenner continued working at the Institution of Electrical Engineers in Savoy Place in London. I had now been hired by CBC Radio, based in Little Titchfield Street near Oxford Street, and was enjoying everything about my new job, including the commute. Each morning I would board the train at Beaconsfield, which was the nearest station to Winchmore Hill, and only a few kilometres away. It was always source of amusement to me how everyone just politely took a seat with barely a "Good morning" to the person sitting right beside. Then out would come the news-papers. Kenner taught me how to fold them into a tall for-mat that allowed you to turn each page in such a way that you didn't bump elbows with the person next to you. All the way to London the train was full of silent people holding up these narrow newspapers. It was so precise, so dignified and, to me, so British.

Once I left the train at Marylebone Station I had a twenty-minute walk to Oxford Street. My route took me down Baker Street and I always looked for the sign for 221B, the fictional address of Conan Doyle's Sherlock Holmes.

On the days I was not working at CBC I would bustle around the house in Winchmore Hill, cleaning, cooking, enjoying domestic life. Winchmore Hill was really just a hamlet, but it was as sweet as its name. The village square was actually a triangular green, with a combination general store, butcher shop and post office. Just around the corner from the square was the village pub, The Plough.

Kenner was his usual attentive, loving self. We would go for walks in the evening, church and a special lunch out on Sundays. But I could still feel my rising doubts about what he was really up to. The conflicting thoughts continued creating a quiet argument in the back of my brain, and I lived with an undercurrent of internal tension.

Was he really the person he seemed to be? What about his unwillingness to discuss or share responsibility for our family finances, and that strange display of participation in military service? I had eventually challenged him on that, somewhat gently, and his only response was to give up attending Naval Reserve meetings, claiming they were requiring too much time away from me. Was he just a harmless eccentric or a fraud? I had no answers. I couldn't prove that he was telling me the truth—and I couldn't prove that he was lying.

Early in the new year the phone rang in the evening and Kenner answered it. I could hear him engaged in a lengthy and apparently amiable conversation. When it ended, he explained that James, his friend from Ashwell prison, was coming to visit next weekend with his wife, Anne. James, he reminded me, had been his one true friend during that time—a gregarious Yorkshireman who had mishandled funds while managing a bank.

When they arrived, I watched in awe as two very large people extracted themselves from a compact car.

"James!" Kenner looked like a child as they greeted each other. His hand disappeared in the grasp of his gigantic friend.

The visit was a huge amount of fun. James and Anne were wonderful company. They were friendly, entertaining and thoughtful houseguests. I can't remember ever laughing as much as I did that weekend. As the time came to leave, they squeezed themselves into the car. James turned the key in the ignition, but instead of a healthy rumble of readiness, the result was an unsatisfactory whining sort of effort from the engine.

With a look of chagrin and a half-smile, James glanced at us and then turned his attention back to the dashboard and the key. Again and again he tried—to no avail. Then suddenly his geniality disappeared, replaced by rage. I instinctively took a step back, frightened by what I saw.

He was now screaming at the car. He doubled up his massive fist and smashed it through the dashboard. The act was shocking, scary and lightning fast. Eventually the car did start and he and Anne drove off. But my lasting memory of James wasn't of his friendliness and fun but, rather, of a huge, powerful man who was easily provoked into anger and violence. I would soon have reason to remember this.

On the first of March the Welsh celebrate St. David's Day. The patron saint of Wales died on that day in AD589. Dewi Sant, as he is known in Welsh, was educated in Cardiganshire, and founded religious houses across Wales and in England. He went on pilgrimages as far as Jerusalem, where he was made an archbishop. Many miracles are

Primrose and John on their wedding day.

Primrose and Kenner. She looks happier here, with her delightful little boy.

I see confidence and defiance in Kenner's face. The child seems completely unintimidated.

Kenner stands beside Billy the bull. This was apparently a risky thing to do, but Billy behaved like Kenner's pet.

Kenner's resumé included "Crucifer to His Royal Highness, the Prince of Wales" —
which was true. Here he is en route to the Investiture at Caernarfon Castle.

Kenner as Liberal Party agent in Sheffield, Yorkshire. He was described in local newspapers as an up-and-coming political force.

Weybridge
10.5.82
may

Hi Dai!

After our telephone conversation yesterday, I thought that I had best do some quick action today so as to allay your concern — and to cheer you up a little. By the way, you're not getting pre-wedding nerves or anything are you? No! second thoughts? No, I hope not!!!

My first three actions on getting to the office this morning:—

1) Make coffee
2) Rang R.B. of Canada and cancelled my application for a Home Ownership Scheme bond. Instead I won't do anything so permanent until your note. In the meantime, I've bought 5000 × £1 Municipal Growth Loan shares in the City of Liverpool @ 14 3/4%. That way we can discuss the long term use of the

My fiancé Kenner writes to say he's invested the money I saved and sent from Canada—about twelve thousand dollars—in high-interest bonds. He hadn't.

Kenner's pen, which he handed me to sign the visitors' book when we first met. When we parted for the last time, I found he had left it behind.

Walking down the aisle with my step-father in the tiny church in Lantzville on Vancouver Island.

Out of the church and into the car in a light sprinkling of summer rain. I could not have been happier.

Diocese of British Columbia
Marriage Certificate

This is to certify that

KENNER ELIAS JONES

of **WEYBRIDGE, SURREY, U.K.**

and

DONNA LEE MACKENZIE

of **NANAIMO, B.C.**

Were United In
Holy Matrimony

in **ST. PHILIP'S-BY-THE-SEA, LANTZVILLE B.C.**

on **JULY 3RD 1982**

by **THE REV'D MARTIN DOHM-SMIDT**

Witnesses **Carol Bell**

John Jackson

I Certify the above to be a true extract from the Register of Marriages kept in **LANTZVILLE, B.C.**

this **3RD** day of **JULY** A.D. 19 **82**

Martin Dohm-Smidt

Incumbent or Officiant

The wide nib and turquoise ink are unmistakably those of Kenner's pen, which he proudly handed to the witnesses and priest. Years later he told a BBC Wales reporter he had never met me.

Pictures from Kenyan TV

For seven years from 2003, Kenner, who has no medical qualifications, posed as a doctor in Kenya and took children into his care. He set up a charity there, Luke's Fund, and used it, as ever, to steal money and destroy trust.

In 1991 the Vancouver Sun reported: "A Welsh man with a criminal record in three countries including 55 convictions in Britain is fighting a deportation order from Canada on the grounds he's been rehabilitated through friendship with a 76-year-old blind Vancouver woman."

attributed to St. David. It is said when he was preaching, he caused the ground to rise beneath him so that everyone could see and hear him.

One of the national symbols of Wales is the daffodil. It got to be that in a roundabout way. The leek, a long, green, onion-like vegetable, became the Welsh symbol when soldiers going into a major battle were told by their leader to wear leeks in their caps so they could tell friend from foe. The Welsh word for leek is similar to the word for daffodil, so there was a bit of confusion. Eventually the daffodil became a national symbol, too.

Going home from work on St. David's Day, I arrived at Marylebone Station with time to spare. Each day I'd see this lovely old lady sitting on the platform, surrounded by buckets of flowers. We were watching our pennies, I believed, so I didn't often splurge. But today was an exception. I bought five bunches of daffodils before boarding the train for home.

During the journey I practised my Welsh and thought about my life. We still hadn't begun to search for a house. Kenner explained that the City of Liverpool bonds he had purchased for us with the money I'd sent from Canada were being held longer than expected. I didn't really know what that meant and I had decided not to push it. He had insisted at the beginning of our marriage that he would handle all the banking and the household accounts. He became grumpy if I questioned things. There always seemed to be enough for food and rent, and that seemed reasonable, as both of us were working.

I pushed any concerns aside because I had something more important on my mind: I was sure I was pregnant.

Part of my dream when marrying Kenner was to have a family. I had five children lined up in my imagination. I could see their shoes by the front door. I had a house filled with laughter, music, love. I desperately wanted a baby and now I was certain one was on the way because I could feel the presence. There was something about the energy, the warm sense of life and excitement.

We had decided that if ever we had a boy, we would name him Risiart, the Welsh version of Richard and a name that Kenner loved. But I knew this was a girl. I was going to name her Robin. For now, though, I would have to be patient. I didn't want to bring Kenner the news until a doctor confirmed it. I had an appointment coming up.

When I got into the station, Kenner was waiting. As I stepped down, laden with yellow blooms, he began walking toward me.

"Dydd gwyl Dewi Sant hapus, cariad! Happy St. David's Day, sweetheart," I said, smiling and holding out the armload of daffodils.

I had been concentrating so hard on my surprise gift of flowers and getting the Welsh right that I hadn't really noticed that Kenner was staggering a bit. He looked flushed. He had never met me like this before. In fact, I'd never seen him drunk.

"What's going on?" I asked when he came close. "You smell of whiskey."

He gave me a half-hearted smile as he saw the daffodils. "Oh, very good. For St. David's Day."

The fun of the moment had vanished. I was worried.

"What's happening, Kenner? Listen, give me the car keys. You're not driving like this." I handed him the armload of flowers and took the keys from him. "You're going to have to explain what's going on." We walked to the car.

"I'll explain later," he said. "It's Friday night. Let's just have a good weekend and I'll tell you all about it on Monday."

As I drove us home, my heart was aching. "Come on, what's going on?"

"Let's just have a lovely few days and I'll tell you all about it later."

"No. Tell me now. I'm not waiting until Monday. There's something wrong and you have let me know what it is. What is it?"

"I've written it all in a letter for you and I'll give you the letter on Monday."

"A letter? I don't need a letter. I need you to tell me right now."

I couldn't get another word out of him. When we arrived home, he required my help getting out of the car, into the house and onto the bed. There he passed out. I pulled off his shoes, covered him with a blanket and began to search.

A letter, a letter. Where would he put a letter? Nothing in the bedroom. I checked all the drawers and cupboards. A sideboard stood in the entry. We kept various things there, including what small stock of liquor we had. The whiskey bottle that had only just been purchased and had been full the day before was nearly empty. I rummaged through the drawers and came across an envelope addressed to me. I sat down on the chair by the hall table and opened it. There was the familiar handwriting, the bold turquoise ink:

This is going to be a long and rambling note. It is not going to be easy to write. Please do not stop until you have read it all through.

My life has not been the same since you came into it. I did not think it possible that I could find the kind of love I share with you.

Let me go back a bit. For over 12 years my life was dedicated to politics. I was uniquely successful. I walked the corridors of power and was tempted many times to stray over the ill-defined line which separates bending the rules and breaking the law. I never did stray over. After all these years I had to make a fundamental choice. I could go ahead, probably enter Parliament or work as a senior official at the EEC, the UN or some such body, or I could quit the political scene.

I could not stay as I was. Pressures were being put on me by senior and influential people— Giscard d'Estaing, Soares, Genscher, etc.—to move out of the back stage and move into the public lime-light. My fellow agents were jealous of my contacts. I had to go up or drop out. I decided to drop out.

Why? you ask. Well, the cost of fame is all too often paid with one's self-esteem, one's independence, even one's soul. I have seen too many good men turn when the public's glare shone on them. Fame and high regard among one's peers is one thing, but public adoration is another. I thank God that I had the courage to say no to the adulation of 'power'. I wanted to be who I was—not what the backroom boys made of me. I had spoiled too many good men by moulding them into a saleable package to want it done to me.

I was wealthy then—politics can be a lucrative business. I lavished money on friends—most of whom never repaid their loans—and a mother who was given everything she asked for. In 1976 I had over 100,000 pounds in my bank. By 1979 I was left with under 1,000 pounds. Oh, I had creditors totalling over 40,000 pounds but I never saw more than a couple of thousands of it. My conscience is a lot clearer than that of a number of my relatives and so-called friends of that time.

Then I met you. I knew the moment I saw you that we were to be wed. No one deserves you, me less than many. Your eyes glow with kindness. You overflow with care, love, simplicity. It shows in your smile how good, truly good, a person you are.

Never, never, never will I leave you in soul, even if we may be parted in body. When we are both at God's right hand, I will leave you only to thank our Father for showing you to me.

You were not yet touched with the feelings which were in my heart, and I was afraid to tell you of them. If I had lost you, then I could not have faced the future. A feeling within me told me to bide my time.

I started work with British Leyland. Again, my unlearning stupidity let me down. I lent money to friends, acting as a middleman between them and a holiday company. They ran off with the money, leaving me with a fraud charge. My world seemed all darkness. From a leading international politician to a convict in under a year! Only the sure knowledge that you were there kept me going.

Prison—I'm not going to talk about that. I'll say just this. I'll never go back. You kept me going then, Don. Your letters, your care, your love and the certain knowledge that you were to be mine.

When I came out, I decided that I must pull myself up by my laces. No feeling sorry for myself— the wronged innocent bit. I would still succeed in life. Sure, I lied about my past, covered up my time in prison, but I did get a job. It didn't pay highly, but it got me by.

Now I felt confident to pop the question. You said yes, of course. I'll tell you this now, Don, whatever happens in our lives, insofar as I have a choice, I'll always go the way which I feel will hurt or harm you least. Nothing will ever come between us, but also nothing will be allowed to put you through the agonies I experienced three years ago.

Now comes the crunch. I am finished now, my dear Don. I cannot go through all this again. You have your family to support you and I am ever thankful to God for that. I must somehow get you away. I never really deserved you and it is time that my year of bliss ended. You must return to Canada.

Why this now, you ask. I have been blackmailed regarding my past. The man involved has nothing to lose. He has lost his job and now lives on me—or did. He will not threaten me again. I had some rough friends who owed me favours. I called them last week and my blackmailing friend has a rearranged face, two broken hands and a fear which will make me forever safe. But too late.

By last week James—yes James—had milked me of 25,000 pounds. Up to that sum I thought it worth trying to keep him satisfied to safeguard my job and future references. When he asked me for more I called a stop and called in my indebted friend.

How did I pay James? Believe it or not, American Express. I issued a fraudulent cheque— something I learned at Ashwell. Within a few days AmEx will know and the police will call.

I cannot ask you to face this. Indeed, I cannot face it myself. I am going to send you back to Canada after this weekend, a last weekend together. Then I shall face the situation without dragging you through the mire.

I love you, darling Donna. I didn't want this for you. Please forgive me. I should not have forced myself into your life. Go now, please, and make a better life for yourself. My only regret is that now there'll never be a Risiart.

Your devoted, Kenner

CHAPTER 8

A Waking Nightmare

How to absorb what I had just read? All our money gone? Sending me home? Marriage over? Blackmail? I knew that Kenner had not declared his criminal record to his employers at the Institution for Electrical Engineers. I didn't blame him. Jobs were hard to come by in Britain. So the threat of having his past revealed and losing his job was a genuine concern.

And James. How could this be? I believed what Kenner said in his letter. If there was a nudge of doubt, it was overcome—as it usually was—by thinking that no one would invent something like this. A person who truly loved you would never create such anguish and fear. Would he? No. No, he had to be telling the truth. Perhaps this, now, was the explanation for his strange behaviours and his dodging financial questions.

I went into the bedroom and shook Kenner. "Wake up. Wake up. Come on, wake up."

Kenner roused himself. He saw the letter in my hand. I spoke first.

"I've read this." My tears began to roll. "What do you mean, send me back to Canada? And what's all this about blackmail? All our money is gone and we're in a lot of trouble? Tell me."

Kenner answered me sleepily. "Don. You've read it. So you know now what happened. I didn't know what to do. I couldn't tell you."

"You sent someone after James? Is that right? James?"

"It's worse than that, Don." Kenner's speech was slow and slurred. "Oh yes, the same James who stayed in our house. The day after he returned to Yorkshire he called me at work. He said I had a nice little wife and a nice little life, and if I wanted to keep them, I was going to have to pay. If I didn't, he'd go to my employers and reveal that I have a record. And now he's furious. He called me today. He says he knows I sent the person who beat him up. He says now he's coming to kill us. Believe me, I've seen him in action in prison. You have to get out of here. Don, you have to get away."

He wobbled, fell back on the bed and passed out again.

The scene running through my mind was James's fury when the car wouldn't start and his giant fist smashing right through the dashboard. The immense strength and violent temper; it was easy to visualize him coming through the door, bent on revenge.

I didn't know what to do. I couldn't call the police because they would have to be told the whole story. Kenner's connection to James began in prison, so Kenner's record would come out and he very likely would lose his job. We couldn't risk that.

We had no friends, no contacts who might help. With trembling hands, I picked up the phone book and looked for the number for Father Richard, the priest at the local Anglican church we attended every Sunday.

When Father Richard answered the phone, I tried to explain through my tears that I needed help and didn't know where to turn. A short time later he knocked on the front door.

Father Richard was in the last years of his working life and suffering from the early stages of Parkinson's disease. He walked with difficulty, leaning heavily on two canes. After looking in on Kenner, still asleep, he sat and listened while I explained as much as I could. Then I handed him the letter, which he read carefully in silence. When he came to the end, he sighed deeply and looked up.

"This is very troubling. You are right to be concerned. I am concerned, too," he said.

"What should we do?" I asked. "I don't think I can call the police, because then everything will come out. And James is on the way. Kenner, as you saw, has passed out. I'm scared and I don't know what to do."

Father Richard looked into my stricken face.

"The lawyer for the parish is away until tomorrow," he said. "When he comes back, I'll bring him right over here and we'll figure things out. Until then, there isn't anything you can do. You're right not to call the police. That would start a chain of events that would do a lot of damage. No. No, I think you're just going to have to make it through the night until I can bring the lawyer over."

Make it through the night? How was I supposed to do that?

"You're going to have to defend yourself and your home, my dear," said Father Richard. "I would stay with you, but in the state I'm in I would probably be more of a hindrance than a help."

"Defend myself with what?"

"We have to find you something," he said.

We searched the house and the only thing that vaguely resembled a weapon was the iron fire poker.

"Stay awake and be ready in case he comes," said Father Richard. "I'll check on you in the morning and bring the lawyer with me as soon as I can."

He gave me a hug and left. As I watched him hobble away on his canes, I felt abandoned. Surely he could have just stayed with me. Sat with me. Talked with me.

I was on my own in the dark house, my husband in a drunken sleep.

I sat in the hallway with the fire poker in my hand, imagining the enraged giant storming through the door. I fought down my feelings of despair and did the only thing I could think to do: I called my mother. With shaking hands, I dialed the number at the farm in Nanaimo. One ring. Two rings. Three. Four. More. No answer. I hung up. I put my elbows on my knees, my head in my hands and imagined my mother's face.

"Mum. Get to the phone," I said quietly. "Mum. Get to the phone." I visualized her coming into the house while the phone was ringing and picking it up. "Mum. Get to the phone."

I waited about fifteen minutes and dialed again. This time she answered.

What I learned later was that during my first attempted call, Mum was across the farm at my sister Maureen's. Concrete had been poured for a house foundation and a recent rain had flooded the forms. Although the morning sun had dried the fields and roads, the deep channels in the foundation still held water. Mum and Maureen were sweeping vigorously, swishing out the remnants of the rain. Suddenly Mum threw down her broom and ran for her car.

"Are you okay?" Maureen called. "Where are you going?"

"I've got to get to the phone," Mum answered as she headed for her car.

"Why?"

"I don't know. I've just got to get to the phone."

"Use my phone," Maureen said.

"No. I've got to get to the house. I've got to get to the phone."

Mum started the engine and raced across the farm, raising a cloud of dust behind her. As I made my second call, she was just walking in the door.

"Hello?"

Oh my God, she was home!

"Mum. It's Donna." I tried to keep my tone calm, but hearing my mother's voice opened the floodgates.

"What's wrong?" she said. "What's happened?"

I took a deep breath and explained everything. I told her about the letter, about James. About the priest agreeing that there was a huge problem and danger.

"I'm coming," she said. "I'll call you right back."

About a half hour later she did call. Somehow in that time she'd managed to get flight reservations, and she gave me the date and time of her arrival in London. She would be at Heathrow on the next available flight. I could hang on, knowing she was on her way. So now I just had to make it through to the morning.

"This night is your Garden of Gethsemane," Father Richard had said to me as he left. "You have to get through this, and you'll have to do it by yourself."

I moved the chair around so I could see the front door. Then I took a firm hold on the handle of the fire poker, willing myself to swing with all my might if James stormed in. It was a long, lonely, silent vigil.

As the hours wore on, the waves of disbelief and stress gave way to pure exhaustion. I could feel imbalance in every cell of my body. My mind was struggling between looking for explanations and looking for a strategy, a plan. Neither was there. My body was wrestling with a combination of a deep, sore feeling in my core and a feeling of floating. It was as though I was watching someone else's life—surely this wasn't me.

As the hands of the clock moved into the early hours of morning, I became aware that more than my heart was hurting. There was also a growing achy, cramped feeling in my abdomen. The dull pain became sharper. I abandoned my post by the door and headed for the bathroom. I was bleeding heavily. I knew what was happening.

I remember realizing I would lose the baby, my little girl, my Robin. There was nothing I could do about it. I told myself that when my life settled down, as it surely would, we could try again and she would be back—this time for good.

I tried to go back to my seat by the door, but I was too desolate, too tired and too heartsore. I crawled into my side of the bed. Kenner didn't wake up. He never moved. He never knew.

CHAPTER 9

Help and Horror

I have always loved airports. To me, airports are doorways to adventure. They hum with people and business. I love them the most when I have a suitcase in one hand and a ticket in the other. But not this time. This time I was standing against a wall in the arrivals lounge at London's Heathrow. I was leaning for support, too weary to stand up on my own. I was watching the monitor for notification that Mum's plane had landed. Any moment now I knew I would see her. All I wanted was for her to put her arms around me.

There she was, all four-foot-eleven of her. Seeing her walking toward me with her arms outstretched, was like being rescued. I held on tight. She let me weep a bit.

"Okay. Come on, now. You're not alone." She wiped my tears as she did when I was a little girl.

"Come on. Gather yourself and let's go. God never gives you more than you can handle."

I nodded. With our arms around each other, we headed for the Underground train and eventually the house at

Winchmore Hill. As we travelled, I tried to explain as best I could what I knew and understood of the situation, but in doing so, it became clear my tale was filled with more holes than story. It was so obvious how much I was in the dark, how much I had not seen or had chosen not to see. But there was no point in feeling sorry for myself or apologizing for my naïveté.

When we arrived at the house, Kenner was not there. Instead he had left a note saying he was visiting some cleric to pray and get spiritual guidance. My patience had worn thin. Mmm-hmm, I thought. Mmm-hmm.

Eventually he returned. It was difficult to define his demeanour as he came through the door. Not really contrite. Not defensive. He was behaving almost as if none of this was really his fault, that somehow he was the victim.

Father Richard had planned to check on me the morning after my vigil, but on hearing that Mum was on the way had decided, instead, to come back the following day with the parish lawyer for a family meeting. Now we all sat down and tried to figure out the best course of action.

The lawyer suggested that Kenner go to the head office of American Express and make arrangements to pay off the huge balance. Kenner only now explained that he had tried to hold off American Express by writing cheques against what was owing. The cheques were drawn on our household bank account, which was not only empty but in the red. Kenner never did explain how else he'd managed to use the card to obtain money for James. I suspected he purchased goods and then sold them for cash. He wouldn't talk about it, saying he was "protecting" me. And if he wouldn't tell me, he certainly wouldn't tell the police.

In the conference with the lawyer it was agreed that involving the police would be a mistake because it would surely lead to the loss of Kenner's job. It was also decided that the lawyer would contact a private investigator and try to find James before James found us.

A few days later, Kenner and the parish lawyer went to the American Express head office. Kenner assured us all afterwards that arrangements for repayment had been agreed at the meeting.

The investigator found no trace of James and he never did arrive.

After about two weeks in England, Mum was scheduled to go back to Canada. So there we were, at the airport once more. I was torn between opposing feelings: almost a desperation at being alone again with what seemed like a mountain of problems, countered by a resolve to tackle them all head-on and get through to the life I wanted.

I know Mum was putting on a brave face as she waved goodbye.

And so I was on my own. I could sense hopelessness attempting to worm its way into my mind. But through it all, maintaining his innocence, Kenner managed to keep up his side of the story.

Whenever I tried to talk the situation out with him, he would simply say that James was the cause of it all and his, Kenner's, only failing was that he had not handled the pressure well. He would not admit that he should have told me at the beginning, and instead claimed to be a bit old-fashioned about protecting his wife and family from troubles and stress. When I insisted on being treated like an equal, he would shrug and say he just wasn't brought up that way, and wasn't willing to change.

He would gloss over my fears and deep hurts by putting his hand on the side of my face and saying he couldn't live without me and just wanted to give me the life he felt I deserved. I had no response to this.

I recovered my composure enough to go back to work at CBC Radio in London. On my first day back I was sitting in my office, when the phone rang.

"Hello."

"Hello. Is this Mrs. Jones?"

"Yes." I didn't recognize the man's voice.

"Mrs. Donna Elias Jones?"

That now-familiar sharp anxiety began to rise inside me. "Yes. Who is this, please?"

There was a pause at the other end of the phone. "This is the manager at the Royal Bank of Canada. I'm sorry—I was just surprised to hear your voice. I thought you were in Canada."

Yes, we had opened an account at the Royal Bank of Canada in London. It was never used, just opened and left there. But I was baffled. I waited for an explanation.

"The reason I'm calling, Mrs. Jones, is there are some cheques here that have been denied for insufficient funds. They have your name on them."

"What?"

Raw panic swamped me from head to toe. I started to shake. I tried to gather myself enough to respond.

"What are you talking about?"

"Mrs. Jones," said the bank manager, "I think you had better come down here and talk to me. I'll be expecting you."

"I'm on my way."

With a trembling hand I replaced the phone, and then I sat there, staring at the wall. My boss, Doug, happened by the door. One glance at me and he came right in.

"What's up? What's wrong?"

He sat down across from me. Tears were pouring down my face and I shook like a leaf. "Oh, Doug, I could tell you, but you probably won't believe me."

"Tell me," he insisted.

He listened without interrupting as I outlined what had been going on and then told him about the phone call moments before.

"Right," he said. "You're not going alone. I'm going with you."

We climbed into a taxi and headed for the Royal Bank of Canada at Trafalgar Square. We were shown into the manager's office. He was a pleasant man in his late thirties. His narrow office had just enough room for his desk and two chairs. Doug and I sat down.

"I have some things here I think you should see," the manager explained.

"We aren't here to say anything," said Doug. "We are here to listen."

I was unspeakably grateful to Doug for taking the lead.

"Right," the manager said.

He lifted the first piece of paper, turned it around and pushed it across the desk toward me. It was a photocopy of a cheque.

"As you can see, this was written for $2,500. You signed it. But there were no funds to cover it."

I was stunned. Yes, it was a cheque written on an old account I had had when living in Windsor back in Canada. I had emptied the account but hadn't closed it altogether. My banking information and the remaining cheques for the account had come with me to Britain and it was all, I thought, tucked away in a file in the house.

Ice *and* heat rushed through me. The shock must have shown clearly on my face. The name was mine, but the handwriting completing the cheque with a fountain pen, signing my name in turquoise ink, was unmistakably Kenner's.

I said nothing.

The manager took another cheque photocopy, and another and another from the file, and laid them across the desk. There were at least half a dozen for amounts ranging from a few hundred dollars to thousands. All rejected. All in Kenner's handwriting.

"Show him your ID," said Doug.

I took out my CBC identification card with my photograph and signature, and other ID cards, as well, and handed them across the desk. The manager looked at them briefly and handed them back.

"This is clearly not your writing or your signature," he said. "Mrs. Jones, you have no idea what's going on here, do you?"

"No. I don't." But in truth, I now had a pretty clear idea.

"What else you do have?" Doug asked.

"Yes, I think you should see the rest of this," said the manager. He pulled out a series of letters:

I appreciate your concerns about this account. I have been waiting for funds from the sale of our house in Surrey, and while I was counting on the amount being deposited by now, the delay has caused this temporary embarrassment. I assure you it will be solved forthwith.

"We have no house in Surrey!" I exclaimed. "What is he talking about?"

"I'm sorry. It gets worse," said the manager:

Under no circumstances are you to contact my wife with any concerns about the status of this account. Her health is very delicate and she can stand no stress whatsoever. Know that if you contact her, it will likely be more than she can bear. Any deterioration in her health will be your responsibility. Please deal only with me.

Another letter:

There is no point in you attempting to contact my wife. Her health condition has become so grave that she has been forced to return to Canada for specialized treatment that will hopefully save her life.

I was reading this utter nonsense through a screen of tears and shock. After all that had happened, all the promises and assurances that the damage done, allegedly by James and the blackmail incident, was now behind us, this had surfaced. I could hardly breathe.

"I know now that you are not part of this," said the manager. "It really was just on a whim that I picked up the phone this morning. That's why I was startled to hear you. I had believed that you were in Canada and near death."

He tapped the top of the desk with his fingers for a few moments. "And there's something else," he said. "We have been notified that because of the number of bad cheques written on a Canadian bank, the police in Canada have opened a file on you and a warrant has been issued for your arrest. As the cheques were tendered here in Britain, the Canadian branch contacted us to try to get to the bottom of things."

I was trembling again.

"I will be notifying the police that we are satisfied that someone other than you wrote the cheques," he said.

"Thank you for all this," said Doug. "We'll get some advice and get back to you."

"I understand," said the manager.

We all stood and he shook my hand. "I'm sorry, Mrs. Jones. I had a feeling all along that you knew nothing about this. I regret that I listened to his stories and didn't try to contact you earlier."

We were back in a taxi, heading for the CBC.

"Now, listen to me," said Doug. "There is obviously more going on here than you know about. You're not safe. I'm going to get you a ticket to Vancouver. You have to get out of here. You have to go home to your family."

When we arrived back at the office, he did just that. He organized for me to fly the next day. I gathered my things, thanked him as best I could and went back to Winchmore Hill.

Kenner was waiting for me at the train station. He could tell at a glance that something was terribly wrong.

"Don, what's happened?"

I was devastated and furious. I explained what I had seen at the bank. As usual, he had his plausible explanation.

"I had forgotten about that account," he insisted. "It was part of my efforts to get James to leave us alone. I was trying to keep you safe, keep our life moving forward. I didn't want him to take away our happiness and our little family. I just forgot to tell you about it when everything else was going on."

"No," I said. "You promised me you had told me everything. There's a warrant out for my arrest. My good name is in tatters. You forged my signature on cheques. You *forged* it!"

The next morning, heartsick and confused, I flew out of Heathrow.

CHAPTER 10

A Second Chance

Less than a year had passed since I was at the farm on Vancouver Island, fluffing out my wedding dress, dreaming my dreams, walking on air. Now I could barely drag my pathetic, heartsick self into my mother's house. How had I come so quickly from bliss to despair? My heart was so battered it hurt when I took a deep breath. I tried to put on a brave face so my family wouldn't worry.

I wasn't sure how to go on. My dreams were smashed; everything I had worked for had vanished down some bottomless sinkhole I still couldn't explain. I went over and over the conversations we had just before I left. Kenner had responded to my every question, every complaint, with stories of his attempts to save our marriage, our lives, our future. He had constantly presented himself as my protector whose only fault had been well-intentioned mistakes. I truly did not know what to think.

I called Father Martin, who had married us in St. Philips-by-the-Sea. He came to the farm and we went for a walk. In the fields near the house, we trudged back and forth, around and around. I explained everything as best I knew it. He listened all the way through, interrupting only now and then to be sure he understood.

"So what do I do, Father? Do I end the marriage? Do I give him another chance?"

I was confused and embarrassed by the mess in which I found myself.

Father Martin stopped and turned to look at me. "Do you still love him?" he asked.

I reflected carefully before I answered. "I do," I said. Later, in retrospect, I would come to realize I loved the person I *thought* Kenner was, the man I had persuaded myself was real. I was also still in love with my dreams and desperate to make them all come true.

"Here's the thing," said Father Martin. "From what I can tell, you don't know for sure if Kenner is telling you the truth. And you don't know for sure if he is lying." He paused. "You took an oath, made a promise—for better or for worse. Well, this is part of the 'worse,' and because you don't know what the truth is, you have to give him another chance. You're his wife."

I felt a rush of relief. I didn't have to bury my dreams. Maybe there was still hope. My adviser had said to carry on. We walked back to the house.

The path had seemed clear when Father Martin had pointed to it, but after he left, fear replaced my relief. How on earth was I going to manage? And what if Kenner really was just a liar? How was I going to rebuild and recover and pull it all together? It would be up to me.

- - - - -

Kenner answered the phone at our home in Winchmore Hill. I told him I had talked with Father Martin and I wanted to save our marriage and our future.

"You have to listen to me," I told him. "I am willing to try and I will sponsor you in Canada. I can find work here and start paying off our debts."

There was silence on the other end of the phone. "Are you there?" I asked.

"Yes, I am," he replied. "But I don't deserve another chance, Don. I've let you down horribly."

"Yes, you have. That's why you need to understand that this must be the end of the problems."

Even as I said the words, I knew I was far from confident, but I had clung to the idea of being true to my vows, as Father Martin had said. I didn't want to see myself as a quitter. And there was the ever-present thought that I simply could not prove Kenner was lying. I took a deep breath.

"Kenner, you need to pay attention. If one penny, one single penny, ever goes missing or is unaccounted for, if there is ever one more phone call about money problems or overdrawn accounts, we're through. Do you hear me?"

Again a pause. Then, "Don, I know it doesn't look good, but I didn't set out to do anything wrong. I was just trying to save our life together, our family."

I wanted to believe him. I really did. I also didn't want to face the possibility that my judgment was so faulty I had been living a life of lies.

"Well, whatever has happened, it has to stop. Now. If you promise me the problems will end, then you can come to Canada and we'll start over from here."

And so it was agreed.

I found work at a television station in Vancouver and we rented an apartment in North Vancouver. We checked the bus connections, put a modest household together, opened an account at a local bank—and started again.

In the beginning things seemed to go well enough. Kenner was subdued, but strangely still unapologetic. He continued to take the position that things had not been his fault—that beyond mismanaging a crisis he had done nothing wrong. I decided to close that file in my mind and just look to the future. I was making a fair wage and banking any extra, however little that was.

Kenner volunteered at the local office of the Liberal Party. He wanted to connect with the community, he told me. Also, he said that without something to occupy his mind he'd go mad with boredom. After a couple of weeks of spending time at the Liberal office, he seemed to cheer up immensely. I put it down to his love of politics and having a chance to use his brain. He was much better company.

One day he came home with several hundred dollars in his wallet.

"Look, Don!" He was so excited. "They can't pay me officially, but they say they value my work and wanted to give me something for expenses. I'm being paid under the table, so to speak."

I can admit now that my heart clenched. Where had that money really come from? Did the organization really do that sort of thing? Wasn't a volunteer just a volunteer? But again, how to verify what Kenner said? I thought about phoning the Liberal Party office and speaking to someone, but I felt the risk was huge. If it turned out that they really had given him some money for expenses and he found I was checking on him, that would destroy any trust we had, however slender it might be.

"Well, that's great," I said. "Let's put that in the bank and build up some savings."

Kenner said he'd go the next day and make the deposit. Sure enough, he came home with a deposit slip and the account balance noted at the bottom. The amount wasn't much, but it was slowly growing. I dared to let myself hope that things had truly turned for the better. I tried to relax.

One day I playfully tossed a cushion at Kenner while he was reading the newspaper.

He dropped the paper, glared at me and said in an acid tone, "Don't ever, ever, ever do that again."

His face was so horrible, so granite hard, so evil looking that shock ran through every nerve in my body. It was as though an unknown, terrifying person was sitting there, not the man who supposedly loved me. I had seen that face before, the night we walked in the rain in Caernarfon and he turned to look at me with those unreadable eyes and predatory grin.

I sat immobile, saying nothing, trying to calm myself. The shock gradually faded. The memory did not.

Several months passed. I continued working at the television station. Kenner kept up his volunteering, coming home now and again with "expense money" and occasionally with the use of a shared office car, which they were happy to let him borrow. With a note of excitement in his voice, he would tell me of the prominent people he was speaking with at the Liberal Party office: Gordon Wilson, Marc Lalonde, Ray Perrault, all big-name politicians and organizers. Apparently they and others were happy to talk politics, economics and campaign strategies. Kenner was in his element and confident that a paying position was just around the corner for him. It would certainly have been welcome, because with my paycheque alone we were only just managing.

I was home alone one day, when the telephone rang. It was the receptionist at the television station where I was working.

"There's something going on," she said.

"What?" I asked. She was keeping her voice deliberately low.

"The police have been here looking for you."

Every nerve in my body, which had only just dared to feel a bit soothed and normal, sprang back into full-panic mode. My gut hurt, my skin hurt, my heart sank.

"What?" I said again. "What did they say? What did they want?"

The receptionist explained that the police had come with an arrest warrant because they had an unpaid vehicle lease with my name on it and a series of bounced cheques. I quickly scribbled down the names of the police officers.

"It's not me doing this." My words sounded so trite.

"I know it's not you," she said. "I told them I'd try to reach you. They said that was fine. They're not going to your house."

I thanked her, hung up and headed out the door. At the police station I was led into a small interview room. I showed the police officers my passport, driver's licence and any other ID I had on hand. They opened their file and compared my signature with the documents they held. Even before they handed me several pieces of paper, I knew what I was going to see. Kenner's handwriting is unmistakable. Besides, this was nothing new—I had seen examples at the bank in London of his forgery of my signature. Here it was again. My final hope that we had any kind of a future shattered. It was over.

The police agreed that I was not responsible for the lease and the cheques and told me they would remove me from the file as a suspect. I explained that the person they really wanted was my husband and that I was now going to end the marriage. I left it up to them to determine what, if anything, they were prepared to do.

My next stop was the bank in North Vancouver where we held our joint account. Not only was there no money in it, not even the slim savings that I believed were there, but it was hugely overdrawn. Kenner must have been showing me deposit slips and balances that he had faked.

In truth, I can't remember now what I said to Kenner when he arrived home, but I know I made it clear that we were through. I had tears running down my face, but my voice was cold and quiet. I had drawn my boundaries when he came to Canada and he had agreed. I could not live like this. I would not live like this. Kenner left the apartment and didn't return that night. For the first time in all this sad drama, I didn't care.

The next day, I went to work and spoke to my boss, the news director. I explained the situation and he heard me out. I didn't feel I could comfortably continue in the news-room and was too shattered to concentrate properly on my job. My first priority needed to be getting my life in some sort of order and getting Kenner out of my world.

When I got home to the apartment, Kenner still wasn't there. Neither was the vehicle that had supposedly belonged to the Liberal Party office. He had taken some clothes and personal items.

I packed myself a suitcase and boarded a bus for the ferry to Nanaimo.

Before long another letter arrived at my mother's address. It held no surprises. This time I was reading with different vision. Reality had dawned. I felt incredibly stupid:

My darling,

Try to be strong now for I need your strength. The sands of time are rapidly running out as far as my life with you on Earth is concerned. But my faith ensures me that my ever-loving Lord has a place where we may spend an eternity together. In the meantime, I will watch over you for the duration of your temporal existence. You will know that I am always with you.

It was so corny; such oily, pompous garbage. How could I have not seen clearly before? And it felt insulting that he would regard me as so easy to manipulate, but I certainly had been and that was my own fault.

The letter continued:

Forgive me, but the pressures of the past years have finally proved too much. I don't know what is going on any more—only that I have a love for you so strong that I know that I am at last doing the right thing by you now.

A fair brain, a successful past career and a loving wife do not put food on the table. I chose politics again and am suffering—and you with me—for being involved in high-level intrigues. Money problems? Sure, I've kept those from you while promises of money from Ottawa (from the Liberal Party) have never come through. I've played a game with non-existent money while I waited and waited. I've told you lots of lies. We've had no money for two months. But the Marc Lalonde story is true . . .

The story was one he had come home with and I had shrugged off at the time as a perhaps harmless fantasy. He had said Marc Lalonde, a former Liberal Member of Parliament and high-level party executive, wanted to enter into some kind of business arrangement with him. The lie was now obvious. The letter went on:

No Art Lee. No Ray Perrault, just the resurrection of a long-standing relationship with M.L. that he and I developed when he visited Europe over four years ago. Now, despite phoning him tonight, he has to protect his career. He simply had to find a safe way to channel funds to me. Now he won't even admit that I exist.

My little white light has been snuffed out. I cannot ask you to stay with me while I am psycho-analysed, questioned and humiliated. I will not ask you to stay with me while the cell doors in politics—my only real success career—are shut in my face. On the other hand I cannot go on without you. So choices narrow to only one gentlemanly thing to do.

I'll try to make it look an accident so that it will look better. Mother and everyone could cope with that better. I have taken everything in hand. There is nothing of value in the car with me but for my memories of you and my wedding ring. I can leave happy having known you—a real angel on Earth.

When my memory has faded a little, try to make a new life and don't close your heart to another relationship. James sort of won in the end but I don't blame him alone—I just couldn't cope with everything anymore.

I am going to Edmonton now. I want to see the Canadian Rockies about which you have spoken so much. There I shall be close to you again. If possible, I want my ashes scattered on Brannen Lake, by your mother's house, with a few kept for Mount Snowdon, in Wales. That is all I ask now.

Mum was patiently waiting while I finished reading. I'm sure my face carried a wide variety of emotions: anger, sorrow, disgust. I handed her the letter and she read it through. We looked at each other across the room, each of us wondering if it would be inappropriate to laugh. We gave in and howled until we were gasping for breath. It felt wonderful. After we collected ourselves and expressed appropriate outrage, we focused on a simple strategy: just send him back.

CHAPTER 11

Lying to a Liar

Although it had seemed like a far-fetched idea, Kenner did make it from Vancouver, across British Columbia, through the Rocky Mountains to Alberta and the prairie city of Edmonton. He had sent a postcard with just a few words on it, and it carried an Edmonton postmark. We had given a report to the police and asked them to watch for him as a distraught, possibly suicidal person, but he had slipped by everyone and into the neighbouring province.

Kenner managed to find my sister Carol, who was living in Edmonton at the time, and persuaded her to let him stay with her for a few days. We had called to let her know he might be heading in her direction, and had warned her he was unstable and maybe desperate. When he arrived on her doorstep, she called us back as soon as she could, whispering into the phone. She assured us she was not afraid of him, but after he left, she admitted she had been nervous and now slept with a knife under her pillow.

True to a pattern we could now predict, Kenner went to the local Anglican cathedral, met with the vicar and enlisted the cleric's sympathies with some wild fiction.

A card arrived, addressed to me in my maiden name:

> *I began to think that there might be some way out of this yesterday when the Lord gave me a message. I fell asleep at the wheel coming through the Rogers Pass and woke up speeding down the wrong side of one of those divided tunnels. Miraculously, I hit nothing, and nothing came the other way. I went to the cathedral this morning and sat there for ages.*
>
> *I'm not crazy and I'm not going to be treated as 'poor Ken', the burden which the family must carry. So I hope that you will forgive me for seeking my way out and, hopefully, leaving you with freedom and less heartache than I gave you. I just love you so much that I can see no other way.*

The note was signed—strangely—Kenwyn.

I was not equipped in any way to understand what was going on with him, let alone deal with him. I just knew he was sick.

Another letter arrived, again saying he had decided to end it all. He wrote that he parked in an empty lot, took a large quantity of some kind of pills and laid himself down to die. Again some "miracle" occurred and he vomited up the pills—a sure sign, he wrote, that the Lord had plans for him. He said he took the message to heart and would mend his ways, soldier on and win my love and trust again.

I could do nothing more than shake my head. These suicide notes were becoming tedious.

Kenner returned to Nanaimo. When we picked him up at the airport, we took him, with the help of the family doctor, directly to the Nanaimo General Hospital. He was admitted to the psychiatric ward for assessment. After three days the psychiatrist from the hospital, the family doctor and Father Martin came to the house together. We all sat in the living room. The psychiatrist was a middle-aged man with a confident air. I felt that I could trust what he had to say. He waited until introductions were finished then spoke first, directly to me.

"This man is a sociopath. He's a narcissist and a compulsive liar. Nothing you can say or do will help him or change him. Now, listen to me carefully."

The psychiatrist waited until I made clear eye contact with him.

"This man is bent on killing you. If he can't do it emotionally or mentally, I can't rule out that he won't try physically. You must, you *must*, get him out of your life. There is no other choice. Do you understand me?"

I did.

Kenner was discharged from the hospital the next day. It was up to me to tell him that he had to go back to Britain and that our life in Canada together simply could not continue. But how to persuade him to leave? I decided the easiest way was to lie. The irony of lying to a liar was not lost on me. But I suspect it worked because he wasn't expecting it.

"We can't continue the way things are," I began. "Surely you can see that the family here doesn't support you and the situation with the police coming to the newsroom, and all of that, well, it is just a huge mess right now."

Kenner nodded. He didn't say anything. I continued. "I think you need to go back to Britain and get things in order there, find some work so we can start again. In the meantime, I'll find more work here. We have huge debts to pay off and we need to dedicate ourselves to that now."

Kenner just looked at me.

"We won't be apart for long," I said. "And while we are, we can stay connected through prayer." I was shamelessly using his professed attachment to the church. I handed him his Book of Common Prayer and picked up mine—the gift he had given me on our wedding day. I willed tears to spring from my eyes—but in truth it wasn't difficult to summon them, as I was an emotional wreck. "My favourite service is compline—the prayers at the end of the day."

"I know it is, Don. I know you love that service," he said.

"So," I said quietly with a sob in my voice, "every night I will pray compline and I know you will be praying it, too. It will connect us."

This was exactly the sort of thing he would have said to me. It hit home. His face softened. "If you will promise to pray compline with me every night," he said, "then I will go and I will know that we are still man and wife, and we will be together again."

"I will," I said. I had a twinge of conscience at manipulating him like this, but I didn't have the strength to persuade him any other way. I knew that if I used anger or made demands, he would dig in his heels. This gentler approach seemed to be working.

The next day, Mum and I packed him into the car and

headed for the ferry to Vancouver and the international airport. We had a one-way ticket to send Kenner back to Britain. We got him into the car and on and off the ferry. But once we were on the way to the airport he seemed to wake up to what was happening.

"Are you sure you really want me to go, Don?"

His voice was different. I could hear the tone heading toward stubborn and manipulative. I stuffed my real self into a corner.

"It's the only thing to do right now if we want to have a future together," I said. "It's the best plan. And it's not for long, not forever. We'll be in constant contact with each other and make this work."

I didn't dare look at Mum's face. I could only imagine. But I knew she understood completely what I was doing and didn't interfere with the farce.

Kenner was becoming increasingly prickly and uncertain. "Don, I could stay and try to put things right," he said. "Let me try."

"No, I'm sorry, but this is the best for us all."

We carried on down a steep hill and suddenly smoke was pouring out one of the wheel wells. Mum pulled over immediately. I had a membership with the British Columbia Automobile Association for emergency roadside assistance and quickly found a pay phone. We had a limited amount of time to get him to the airport and on the flight we had booked.

"This is a sign, surely," said Kenner. "A sign from the Lord that I am supposed to stay. I'm not supposed to leave you, Don."

Oh God! I pretended I didn't hear him. The BCAA tow truck pulled up behind us. The burly, cheerful driver inspected the car and gave us his diagnosis: overheated brakes. He advised us simply to wait half an hour to let everything cool off and then we'd be fine.

This was good news—and bad news. The good news was we would soon be able to carry on to the airport and be in time for the flight. The bad news was we had to kill time, thirty minutes full of nothing except worry that Kenner would either refuse to go to the airport or simply disappear.

We went to a coffee shop nearby and I did everything I could to appear as calm and supportive as possible. I talked about how we'd be able to pay off our debts and start fresh. I talked about how wonderful it would be to return to Britain to live. I played every dream-weaving mind game I could think of.

At last we were off to the airport again. As we headed for the check-in counter, Mum reached into her purse for the ticket. Kenner decided to try once more to wriggle free.

"Give that to me," he said to Mum.

"No." She kept walking toward the check-in.

Kenner reached across to snatch it out of her hand, but she was ready for him. She swung her arm back, keeping the ticket away from him.

"I said no!" Mum's voice and face were stern.

He made another grab.

"Stop it!" she said, clearly angry.

"If you give me the ticket," he said, "I'm sure you'll be glad to see the back of my coat."

Mum kept her grip on the ticket and firmly placed it on the counter in front of the check-in agent. She and I were both watching in case Kenner tried to take it again. Caught behaving like a child, Kenner calmed down and pretended that this was all good, all his idea. But we weren't going to let our guard down for a second. If he got that ticket, he would run. We knew he would cash it in somehow, and more important would be at large. This was not going to happen. He *had* to leave.

Before long the check-in agent handed Kenner his boarding pass and passport. We watched his suitcase vanish on the luggage conveyor belt. Time was now short. The agent said Kenner needed to head through the security point right away and get to the departure gate. I hugged him goodbye and promised to pray compline that very night. A bit uncertain but nonetheless compliant, Kenner disappeared through the door. But that wasn't good enough. Mum and I decided we could trust absolutely nothing he might say or do.

We waited at the airport until his flight had departed. Then we watched in the main departures lobby in case he had taken himself off the flight and would re-emerge. We even went to the ticket counter a short time later and confirmed that no passengers had decided at the last moment against boarding the flight. We were assured they were all on the plane. Kenner was on that flight—guaranteed.

"I couldn't believe it," said Mum. "When the smoke started to pour out the side of the car, I thought we were doomed."

"Me, too!" We laughed. "That was close."

"No," she said. "I didn't care what happened. He was going to make it to the airport if I had to push him myself in a shopping cart."

My mother would have done just that. We laughed again—at the thought and from pure relief. We put our arms around each other and left the airport.

When we got back home to the farm, I placed a telephone call to Britain. I spoke to a vicar named Tim from the church Kenner used to attend in Walton-on-Thames. Kenner had spoken of Tim and how he had become a good friend. I had never met him. Kenner had written Tim's name and telephone number in our address book. He was the only person I could think of who might be willing to meet Kenner and try to get him help.

I dialed the number in the UK, and when the church secretary answered, I asked for the vicar. Tim came on the line and I introduced myself. I outlined the basic story and tried to impress on him that Kenner had been diagnosed in Canada with serious mental and emotional problems. I explained that he was a danger to others and perhaps to himself and needed professional care.

Tim heard me out and agreed to meet him at the airport and get him some kind of medical or psychological assistance. It was all I could hope for. I trusted that a clergyman was the best person to help Kenner find some road to healing.

That is not what happened. As I learned later, all Tim did was give Kenner a ride from the airport back to Walton-on-Thames. He dropped him on the doorstep of two elderly women, who had no idea what troubles were now coming into their lives.

CHAPTER 12

Breaking Point

I t seemed that every time the phone rang, or a letter came through the mail slot, it was yet another threat of legal action, another complaint, demand for repayment or accusation of my complicity in some sort of criminal web. And these came from all quarters. Friends, business acquaintances and people I had never even heard of all tackled me, as I was the only one left standing. And who could blame them? They had been lied to and their money taken. For the first time I found enough backbone to write and tell Kenner what I now knew, and to let him know that he and I had no future:

> *I have just received a letter from a professional employment company claiming you signed a contract with them and owe them over $6,000 Canadian. I have returned the letter to them.*
>
> *I have also been telephoned by the mother of my friend Wade. She accused me of taking advantage of*

that friendship and leaving him in the lurch for $450. I am trying to contact Wade now to sort things out with him personally. What on earth were you doing borrowing money from him? What did you tell him? I will find out when I get him on the phone. But I am devastated and furious.

Steve also called last night. He is sending me the details of what he feels is rightly owed to him.

These are people who are now bewildered and upset and looking to me for answers. And when the letter arrived from the employment company, it was one more example of something about which you did not tell me. You had said the résumé you received was done as a personal favour from a friend. You did not tell me you had signed a contract. You could have come clean and told me everything before you left. It leaves me wondering how many more lies will surface in the future.

The way I feel now is extremely confused and unsure of anything at all. I am very angry at all the lies you have told me in the past, and angry at the ones that surface now, that you could have at least warned me about. I cannot rest and I cannot believe anything you tell me.

I must face reality and the possibility that you may never change . . . that you have been lying to me more than I ever suspected and that you may be unable to break out of that.

For my own sanity I must go on. And I plan to do what repairs I can to save my own reputation and peace of mind.

If you love me, Kenner, you must do this for me: you must not contact me either at the farm or wherever you think I may be working. I will not try to contact you after this letter. Right now I am very torn and raw inside and my emotions and thoughts are not functioning clearly.

You have to go down this road by yourself, Kenner. I have no means to help you, nor will I try to bail you out any more.

It is up to you to face your responsibilities, and to seek help—medical and spiritual. I pray that you do.

Having come to grips with the realization that the marriage was over, I tried to find ways to limit the damage that Kenner had done. My lawyer, to my great relief, believed my story and set to work trying to help me through some of the chaos. I took his first suggestion in distancing myself from Kenner by heading for the Immigration office in Nanaimo. I needed to remove myself as Kenner's sponsor to Canada.

I was shown into an office and there I met Bill. He was in the last years of his career and had an air of confidence and experience. He also had a touch of Old World elegance about him and was impeccably dressed in a grey suit, complete with vest. He put down the pipe he was smoking.

"So, what can I do for you?" he asked.

Of course he could see the human wreckage sitting across from him. I was obviously someone with a big problem, someone wrestling with herself to keep her composure.

"I want to un-sponsor someone," I said.

Bill looked at me for a moment. "Why do you want to do that?"

I really didn't feel I could go through telling the story, especially as I was feeling like an idiot for landing myself in this tangle.

"Do I have to tell you? Can I not simply remove my support?" The tears were barely hanging back. I'm sure my face was an open book. I was misery itself.

He picked up his pipe, took a moment to tamp in some tobacco then lit a match and drew a few breaths. He looked at me over the bowl of the pipe, smoke curling from it. When he spoke, his tone was that of an uncle, a favourite, safe person.

"Well, my dear," he said. "This is where you have to decide if you can trust somebody."

That's all it took. My heart opened, the tears began to pour and out came the whole story. And as I told it, his face changed. I could see he believed me. The tale was, after all, pretty impossible sounding. By the time I had finished, he was angry.

"Now, you listen to me, young lady," he said. "Finding a way to revoke someone's residency status is very difficult. But we will find a way. We will find a way. I want you to leave this with me now. I'll be in touch."

Back at home, reality was still waiting for me. Kenner was gone, but the mountain of debts and deceptions was still there. For the next week I tried to sort through everything to see where I stood, which obligations were mine and which were not. My lawyer helped me get a clear picture and a strategy. But there were no quick solutions for the money problems and for my emotional state.

I was staying in a basement bedroom. My meagre possessions were stacked in a corner. I felt no hope, could foresee no future. Crushed, I lay down on the bed to try to collect myself, but it was as though the world was collapsing in on me. I remember losing my peripheral vision. Darkness was circling closer and slowly erasing everything. I had the thought that I was dying—that people could die of a broken heart and it was happening to me. I didn't care. It was all too much. I lay there barely breathing, watching the world become just a small image surrounded by black.

Mum walked into the room. How is it that mothers know? She sat on the edge of the bed beside me. She leaned over, put her hands on either side of my face and looked me full in the eyes. "I love you," she said.

I heard her. I saw her.

"You're going to be okay," she said calmly. "You're going to get through this."

I nodded. The dark had started to move away. She kissed me on the forehead and left the room.

I took a few deep breaths and eventually my vision widened. All right, I thought. There's no use feeling sorry for yourself. Just keep moving. Get up and keep moving.

I washed my face, combed my hair and decided to put on some earrings. I went to the debris pile in the corner to find my fabric jewellery roll. It was a soft cloth organizer I had bought many years ago and it held all my adornments. I didn't have much, just some costume pieces, nothing of value. I pulled the roll out of the suitcase and opened it. Nothing. All my jewellery was gone. I couldn't believe it. He had taken everything. *Everything.* My reputation, my earnings, my heart. He had blasted my life apart in a wave of destruction and stopped at nothing. And now he had even taken my poor collection of jewellery.

I was enraged. I pounded up the stairs and into the living room. Mum glanced up.

"Look!" I held out the empty roll. "He even took my jewellery! My junk jewellery!"

"What?" She was as outraged as I was.

"That's it, Mum," I said. "That man will never, never, never take another thing from me. I will not let him hurt me again. That jewellery is the last thing he will ever get."

I was resolved. I would not let him usurp my family, my friends, my reputation. Instead I would find a way to trust and to love and to be happy. It might take a while, but I'd do it. Because while I was unhappy, he was still winning. I was done with that.

Spurred on by my anger, I began to look for work again. I heard about a position coming open in television current affairs at CBC Edmonton and decided that was my best shot. It would get me out of the trouble zone, to somewhere safe, somewhere I could work to repay debts and rebuild my life.

But I no money with which to pay my way there. Everything had gone into getting Kenner out of the country. The only thing of value I owned was my engagement ring. I sold it for enough money to buy a plane ticket to

Edmonton and a warm, winter coat. It was November. It was going to be brutally cold on the prairies.

I stayed with my sister Carol for a few months. She wasn't making much money and couldn't really afford to keep me. So while I waited for the job to come open at the CBC, I needed some support. I went to the local welfare office and applied. With mixed feelings, I filled in the application. How did I find myself in this situation? What on earth was wrong with me that I couldn't take care of myself? The worker in the office kindly reminded me that this was what the fund was really for: people who suddenly found themselves in difficulties and just needed some help temporarily.

I left with a voucher for half of Carol's rent for the month and a few groceries. In my reduced circumstances I had a new appreciation for how difficult it is to eat properly on limited funds. Carol and I tried to stretch our dollars as far as they would go. Payday for her was about a week away and we had already used up my money in spite of being as careful as we could. We had about five dollars between us. There was a store a short distance from the apartment. We wrapped up warmly in our coats, boots and mitts and went to see what we could find.

Walking along a deserted sidewalk, we suddenly came upon a five-dollar bill lying on top of the snow. We shrieked like children on Christmas morning. And there was more. A ten was nearby! And some change! We whooped and hollered and danced. We were rich! Laughing like a pair of fools, we went on a shopping spree. Our twenty dollars bought a week's worth of tuna, instant noodles, some evaporated milk, rice and a few more items. It was like carrying home a feast.

CHAPTER 13

- - - - - - - - - -

Ominous Echoes

Before long I was working again. CBC Television in Edmonton was a kind of sanctuary for me. I was meeting new people, making my way and trying to put my life back on track. The workdays were interesting, challenging and fun. I didn't talk about my personal disaster. I pretended to be normal.

The weekends were difficult because I wasn't distracted by work. So I filled my time the best I could. I did the normal errands and chores. Sunday mornings were for church and I went to the Anglican cathedral. Although in the past I would have preferred becoming part of a smaller congregation, I chose the cathedral because for the moment I needed to be a nobody in a big crowd.

To get there, I took the electric train. It was a short ride from Belvedere Station to the Bay Station. It was always a pleasure to disembark at the Bay Station and walk over the mottled blue-and-grey tiles and under the wide, chrome-lined ceiling.

Alone in the station, I headed toward the stairs. On the left, perilously near the edge of the platform, was a bright pink balloon. Its string trailed gently along the tiles as the balloon itself floated just above floor level. The air currents in the station were taking the balloon slowly and inexorably toward the tracks.

I walked over and picked it up in a flash of good citizenship, thinking it might cause problems if it floated onto the tracks. I put it in a nearby rubbish bin. Although the balloon rose gently, the string seemed to cling closely enough to the rubbish to keep the balloon in place.

Up the steps I went to the open street. The bells were ringing from atop All Saints' Cathedral. The air was cool and the morning grey and quiet. Once I was inside the door of the cathedral, an usher handed me a thicker-than-usual service sheet. I thanked him and walked through into the sanctuary. But something wasn't right. The place was crowded and ribbon-tied flowers adorned the sides of the pews. People were milling about and shuffling into the pews. A string quartet played up at the front. I looked quickly at the service sheet.

Inside the first page: "The Holy Eucharist with a Celebration of Christian Marriage. Today. The marriage of the Vicar William Roberts and his fiancée, Shelley."

This was the vicar who had talked to Kenner when he came to Edmonton, supposedly asking for spiritual advice and support. I had spoken to the same vicar when I arrived in Edmonton. I had confided tearfully in him but could tell he believed Kenner's story, not mine. I attended services at the cathedral but didn't seek the vicar's guidance again. Now here I was, expecting a morning of peace and meditation. Instead it was a celebration of marriage.

I had to get out of there. I couldn't sit in the church and watch the bride come slowly and magically down the aisle. I couldn't watch two people who loved each other stand and, with mutual love and respect and anticipation of life, exchange sacred vows. I couldn't think of their future commitment, joys and dreams. I couldn't be there and fill the air with pain and sadness and envy on their wedding day. I just couldn't do it.

So I quickly hurried back through the church and out onto the street. I felt like a deserter, but I knew I'd had no choice. And I wondered: Oh God, why was I hurt so badly? Will I ever get over this?

Back down in the Bay Station, under street level, I needed to hide my pain from the world. The pink balloon had drifted again on the air currents. It was where I'd first seen it, floating teasingly over the edge of the platform. I picked it up and sank my fingers deep into its skin. The balloon burst in my hands and the sound, like a gunshot, rang off the walls of the deserted station.

Christmas was bleak. Edmonton was snowed in and frozen solid. My sister had been invited to spend the holidays with her boyfriend and his family in a rural cabin. Of course I encouraged her to go, saying I wasn't very good company right now anyway.

I was sitting in the dimly lit apartment, watching something mindless on television. It was snowing again and only winter light seeped in. My mind was parked in a place of no thinking, no feeling.

The telephone rang.

"Hi, it's Bill, from the Immigration office in Nanaimo." There was something very fatherly and soothing about his voice. "Is your sister there with you?" he asked.

"No. I'm on my own. She's gone for Christmas."

"Mmm," he said. "All right. Is there any whiskey in the house?"

I thought that was odd. "I'll have to go and look."

"Go ahead," he said.

I checked the kitchen cupboards and found a modest stash of liquor. I went back to the phone. "Yes, Bill. There is whiskey here."

"Okay," he said. "Here's what I want you to do. Go and pour a shot and drink the whole thing at once. Then come back to the phone."

The news must be bad.

"But I can't stand whiskey," I said.

"Never mind. Just do it. Come back to the phone when you're done. I'll be waiting."

I poured myself a shot, knocked it back and returned to the telephone.

"Okay, I did it."

"Now, are you sitting down?"

"I am." I took a deep breath.

Bill explained that he had asked the British government for a copy of Kenner's criminal record.

"But I learned something," he said. "The British authorities won't release a person's criminal record to another country without that person's permission."

This was not good. Our strategy for revoking his landed immigrant status was to prove he had lied on his application when he declared that he had no charges, convictions or prison time in his past.

"However," Bill continued.

The "however" had an upbeat tone. I held my breath.

"I refused to be stopped. I found a way—don't ask me how. I managed to get Kenner's record through a back-door connection. Here we go."

Bill began to read. The list was long:

1973: Sheffield Crown Court, four counts
of obtaining money by deception, one
count of forging a valuable security and
one count of uttering a forged valuable
security. Seven counts total. Guilty.
Sentenced to three years' probation, payment
of compensation, and he must submit to
psychiatric treatment at North Wales Hospital
in Denbigh.

What—1973? I had thought all we were going to get was confirmation of the conviction in 1980 that Kenner had told me about. I was wrong. I don't know if the whiskey was helping, but I was hoping it was.

"Bill, wait a minute," I said. "You mean there is more than the 1980 charges?"

"Much more," he said. "That was just 1973. Obviously the sentence and psychiatric treatment had no effect." He continued:

1975: Central Criminal Court, London, one
count of theft of a chequebook, five counts of

forgery, five counts of theft of money, one
count of taking pecuniary advantage by
deception, four counts of obtaining money
by deception, one count of forging a valuable
security and one count of uttering a forged
valuable security. Guilty. Sentenced to twelve
months' imprisonment.

It was shocking—and yet, how familiar did all this sound? Very.

"Oh my God." That was all I could say.

"We're not done yet," said Bill.

1977: Greenwich Magistrate's Court, one
count of theft of property. Guilty. Probation
two years. Must pay compensation. Required
to receive psychiatric treatment at Henderson
Hospital, Sutton.

"Apparently that didn't work, either, Bill."

"No. It certainly didn't."

1978: Kingston Crown Court, two counts of
obtaining money by deception, three counts
of procuring the execution of a valuable
security by deception and one count of
theft of property. Guilty. Twelve months'
imprisonment suspended for two years.

"Here comes 1980," said Bill, "the one he did tell you about."
When Kenner had written to me years earlier, he told

me he had borrowed money to help some friends and then just couldn't pay it back.

"Nineteen eighty is not what he described it to be," said Bill. He read on from the list:

> Coventry Crown Court, two counts of obtain-
> ing property by deception, five counts of theft
> of property, two counts of obtaining money
> by deception, three counts of procuring the
> execution of a valuable security by deception.
> Sentence fifteen months in prison.

Well. There it was. A story that I'm sure neither of us was expecting.

"You have had a narrow escape," said Bill. "I promise you this: he will be barred from Canada. I will get everything in motion as soon as possible. We don't need him near you, or anyone else for that matter. I'll be in touch."

"Thank you, Bill." I put the phone down and tried to digest what I had just heard. Clearly I was not the first to be taken in. There was little comfort in that.

While I tried to pull myself and my life together in Edmonton, Kenner was supposedly doing the same in Britain. Tim, the priest I had contacted to meet him when he left Canada, never telephoned or wrote.

I had some measure of peace for several months and then a letter arrived from one of two elderly women, Mary and Kathleen, who had taken Kenner into their home in Walton-on-Thames in Surrey.

As I came to learn, Kathleen was apparently uncertain about Kenner, but Mary saw a bruised and beleaguered man who needed a safe and loving home. She not only persuaded herself that she was the perfect person to help him but also, having heard the stories he told, decided it was her duty to berate me for being an inadequate, unloving and insensitive wife. I had filed for divorce and Kenner had been served with documents. Mary took pen in hand, ready for battle.

A series of cards and letters began to arrive in my mailbox:

> *I am Mary Thom, Churchwarden at St. Mary's, Walton-on-Thames, for 30 years. With my friend Kathleen, I have had a home for deprived, battered, abandoned, problem, delinquent children. This is by way of introduction and establishing credibility with you in a professional way, and you are more than welcome to check me out with our vicar, Timothy. On October 30th, Timothy sent your Kenner to us for help with accommodation problems.*
>
> *He told his story in a way that shattered me with the balanced, controlled restraint, which so barely, despite his best efforts, concealed his pain.*
>
> *He related the blackmail situation over his criminal offence—his failure to confide in you about it and the extreme financial problems and debts created by it. Then your return to Canada, his failure to get work—and how humiliating that must have been to him in his pride in himself as provider and protector. His deliberate decision to*

*deceive you into thinking he had a job so that your
career prospects would not be spoiled by leaving it
to you to work as a legal secretary to earn regular
money for you both.*

Well, that was malarkey. What else was coming? I read
on:

*Then his exposure: his despair: Edmonton: your
enormous strength and support in getting him
examined by a psychiatrist. And finally his single
ticket here with the aim of financial improvement
to repay debts and getting help in sorting out the
attitudes in himself that had created the problems.
In his telling he was hard on his faults, his guilt,
his responsibility, and totally loyal to you.*

*He has been living with us ever since. I cannot
praise too highly his efforts to get work and the
way ever since he has set up for himself a most
punishing routine, often working an 18-hour day
to establish himself as a journalist. His one aim
was to secure a contract with a lump sum payment
for you to convince you of his shared concern for
your joint debts and marred reputations. When he
achieved this at the end of February, he was elated.*

A lump sum payment? No money—in fact, no commu-
nication—had come from him at all. More letter:

*I only wish he had tried to convey to you then the
effort that it had caused him, and his motivation*

for you—but then you must know he puts a low value on himself.

Donna, he knows and most bitterly regrets the hurt and anger he has caused you—and it was the greatest pity you did not have time together to work out your anger, for left unexploded it is a destructive and eroding emotion and you must have been left confused, savagely raw, so let down and unhappy.

But I am convinced, Donna, that you will never find anyone who will love you more utterly, completely and totally than he does. So often I notice he is thinking of you when he fiddles with his crucifix or wedding ring, and you should hear the pride in his voice when he speaks of 'my wife'.

I am sure you will never find a better father for the children of your union with him.

What children? I could only imagine the stories he had told this trusting woman.

He would gladly pass up anyone but God for you, Donna. We have tried so hard to keep him 'warm' for you.

Because of my life's work I have seen more in Kenner than most and I firmly believe God sent him to us because of this.

Donna, in no way do I underestimate the pain you have suffered. In fact, I think its very intensity has led you to file the divorce rather than face an opening up of it with renewed contact. But you

have as much to lose and gain as Kenner and I am
sure you could work it out together.
Please feel free, if you wish, to write to me with
the openness I have shown to you.

I put the letter down. Comments and responses to her words had been running in my head through every sentence, every paragraph. He was so skilled at presenting fragments and fabrications and manipulating others' emotions. And really, truly, how dare she take the position that she had the right to counsel me? I decided to not reply. After all, what was the point? It would be my word against his and why on earth would she believe me?

But Mary wasn't finished with me yet. Her written onslaught continued a month later:

You now know Ken's record. Whatever you feel
about that, Donna, he is still the same Ken whom
you chose to marry because of the way he met your
deepest personal needs, with his love, his caring,
his tenderness, his understanding. The past which
has surfaced now would have remained buried,
not to be repeated in his present behaviour, had it
not been for the filthy James. The last episode in
Canada of pretending to be working was bad and
wrong, but not unforgivable, and again would
never have happened had he not felt so exposed
and threatened with you after the James affair.
If you reject him now, because you know what
was previously hidden, you offer him no future
hope, no confidence to clear himself and remain

clear, and you confirm in him his strong under-
lying feeling of worthlessness. He has been pun-
ished by the law. He has been punished in a way
no one deserves to be punished by James. His
punishment continues in his problems with you
and within himself.

Your joint financial problems he has succeeded
in solving through his tremendous efforts, his grind-
ing hard work and shatteringly long hours. Give
him the chance to show you he has changed. Money,
possessions, success have lost their hold on him.

There it was again. She obviously had been told—and of
course believed—that he had paid all debts, sorted all legal
and financial tangles. Pure nonsense, of course.

Given the reassurance of your forgiveness, he can
be liberated from his need to lie.

I trust him totally financially. He knows my
credit card number and though he didn't want to, I
have made him go to the instant money point for
me to draw out on my card. He trusts himself and
knows I trust him.

I felt the impulse to warn this woman not to do any
such thing. That he certainly could not be relied upon to
behave in a trustworthy manner.

Ken leaves us very soon now to take up his new
job overseas. I hate the thought of his being on his
own with this problem hanging over him. Here is

my phone number. You know I will respect your confidence.

Along with the fiction about repayment of debts and solving of money problems, Mary still continued to refer to a single criminal offence. She clearly did not know, as I now did, of his long record and what it contained.

Mary was not intending to allow me peace. Yet another letter:

> *He has been so broken up about the divorce and discouraged about the impossibility of getting his side represented. He really feels strongly on the religious angle of the sanctity and permanence of the marriage vows and also their content 'in sickness and in health'.*
>
> *I expect you feel pretty mad about my shoving my oar in again. I can only say that despite all I know and have seen for myself, I still love him for all his personal qualities and his integrity outside his 'sick' area, and there is nothing I would not do to see him made whole.*

Yes, I was fed up with her "shoving her oar in" and of Kenner being portrayed as the long-suffering heart soldiering on, and me as the cruel partner, more than willing to leave the poor man alone and in despair when it was within my power to save him.

If I ever returned to Britain, I decided I would visit Mary and set her straight. I did eventually do that, and our visit held surprises for us both.

CHAPTER 14

Virginia State Prison

I t was a wonderfully sunny day and we were shooting
a television story in Cochrane, Alberta. What a beautiful place! Just west of Calgary, Cochrane was small
enough to look and feel like a prairie town. The Rockies
ring the horizon, snagging clouds on their ragged peaks.
The dusty fields and scrubby trees, the farms and ranches
made for a place of irresistible charm.

After sampling some of the local ice cream we were now
on the outskirts of the main street in an open field. The production team was setting up the camera and checking the
sound recording, when a woman came walking up as quickly
as she could. She waved a piece of paper and called out, "Is
Lee Mackenzie here? Is Lee Mackenzie here?" I went to meet
her. "Here," she said, panting from her exertions. I thanked her
and, puzzled, opened the paper. It held a short message:
"Call your producer in Edmonton." What was going on?

I used the two-way radio in the production van and contacted the television station. When the producer came on at

the other end, I was expecting something like bad news from home, a crisis or death in the family. That is not what I heard at all.

"I've had a telephone call," he said. "I didn't understand it. It was from someone who said he was at Virginia State Prison in the United States. He asked me if Lee Mackenzie was alive or dead."

This made no sense to me. Who? What? "Is that all?" I asked. "Did you get his name and telephone number?"

"No, I didn't."

I had no idea what this was about and I puzzled over it through the rest of the day. When I got back to Edmonton, I learned a second person had phoned, again from Virginia State Prison, asking exactly the same question: "Is Lee Mackenzie alive or dead?" This time the caller left a name and telephone number.

At home, in the quiet, with a pen and paper handy, I phoned Joe. I never did meet him face to face, but we had a long telephone conversation that day. Joe had a deep, melodious voice with kindness in his tone.

"Are you the person who called my place of work?" I asked.

"Yes, I am, and I'm sure you're wondering why."

This was going to be interesting.

"I certainly am," I said. "And as I am here, alive and well, I'm ready to listen. But you have to admit, it's a strange question to be asked."

"I can explain," said Joe.

"But first, why are you calling me from Virginia State Prison?"

"I understand you are married to Kenner Jones," he said.

"I was. But we are divorced."

"Oh." A pause. "That's not what I heard."

"That doesn't surprise me at all." Yes, here it comes, I thought. What story was I going to hear now?

"Joe," I said, "take your time. You go first and tell me everything and then I will fill you in."

Joe began his story. As a lifelong member of the Baptist Church, he included in his spiritual commitment the facilitating of a weekly Bible study group in the prison. He also offered his services as a visitor and counsellor for inmates. As convicts were brought in to Virginia State Prison, they would be added to the list of counsellors such as Joe who did this kind of ministry. Kenner had been put on Joe's list.

KENNER. ELIAS. JONES.

7. SNOWDON. STREET.
CAERNARVON.

XMAS. 1957.

Y BEIBL CYSSEGR-LÂN

SEF

YR HEN DESTAMENT

A'R

NEWYDD

LLUNDAIN
Y GYMDEITHAS FEIBLAIDD FRYTANAIDD
A THRAMOR
146 QUEEN VICTORIA STREET, E.C.4

Kenner's Welsh-language Bible.

"I liked him right from the start," said Joe. "Kenner joined the Bible class and was very knowledgeable. He knows the Good Book up, down and sideways."

Joe said he also visited privately with each of the inmates assigned to him. He would go to their cells and they would talk and pray together.

"Ken," he said, "is one of the most interesting people I have ever met. Sincere. Intelligent. He settled in quickly to life in the prison and decided to make the best of it."

Joe went on to explain that Kenner had been appointed to work in the prison kitchen. "He really knew what he was doing in there. He organized things, and came up with menus that were much better than what the men had been used to eating. The prisoners started to take notice."

The library service also received Kenner's scrutiny. Joe described how he managed to streamline the system to make it more efficient and how he brought in better reading material.

"He even began tutoring some of the prisoners," said Joe. "He would go around and assist some of those who were trying to get their diplomas for high school or were doing other courses. He was helpful, smart and funny. They loved him."

Joe noted that Kenner really opened up in private conversation.

"He told me the whole story about you, your children and how he came to be in prison."

I took a deep breath. I had been keeping notes as Joe spoke. The pencil hovered above the paper as I absorbed again the statement that Kenner was telling the world we had children we did not have. Soon I was racing along again, keeping up to Joe's story.

"He explained that you married him in 1980 and have two small boys," said Joe.

There was no point in interrupting Joe to tell him we were married in 1982. I would get my chance later.

"Go on," I urged.

"Kenner had the chance to come to the United States to work as a political journalist. He told me he was hired by the Canadian Broadcasting Corporation and was going to be their top reporter in the US, but they wanted him to start at the grassroots level. So he went to Leesburg, here in Virginia.

Leesburg, Virginia. Why would he choose to go there? I wondered. Why not a major centre like Washington, Chicago, New York?

"Kenner shipped his car and his things from Britain," said Joe. "He said that when everything arrived, the shipping company gave him the bill. He said the CBC had agreed to pay it as part of his moving expenses. Kenner said the CBC suddenly said it wouldn't pay and he didn't have the money to do so himself, so the shipping company took him to court."

How interesting.

"Kenner said he was working on Walter Mondale's election campaign in California when he was summoned to court. Once Kenner got there and the judge learned he was involved in politics, the judge sentenced him harshly. Kenner said it was more a political move against him than a legitimate legal conviction. The judge threw the book at him and sentenced him to nine years for nonpayment of his debt."

This was another example of Kenner mixing stories and the listener just accepting what he said. After all, what would a reporter on the East Coast of the US be doing working for a presidential candidate in California? But I had been as guilty as anyone of not paying attention to such implausibilities.

Joe carried on, describing how shocked and desperate Kenner felt at finding himself behind bars for the first time in his life. Kenner told Joe that he had, of course, contacted me, his wife, to tell me of his plight, but I was not sympathetic. He said that while he was stuck in prison, I packed up the family home in Britain and took myself and our two young boys back to Canada. He was crushed that I wouldn't respond when he tried to contact me. I wouldn't let our sons communicate with him. He was desolate, heartbroken, baffled. But, soldiering on, he buoyed himself up with his faith and began a campaign to win me back.

"He wrote to you every week," said Joe. "And they were beautiful letters." Joe explained that Kenner had a typewriter in his cell. "When I'd come for my weekly private prayer visit, Ken would give me the most recent letter for you. He'd always ask me to read it over and then mail it for him. He wanted to make sure that he was communicating his thoughts and feelings clearly. And he wanted to be sure the letter didn't get stuck in the prison mail system and not make it out."

Joe said he always agreed to do this. "I'd take the letters home, and my wife and I would read them," he said.

"They were the most tender, sweet letters . . . something you would expect to find in the most powerfully written story, full of love and compassion and the most complete, all-consuming dedication. My wife and I cried openly when we read them. I mailed every single one and you never, ever replied."

"I'll explain when it's my turn, Joe. Trust me—I never received them. Who knows where they really went? And what you have been told is nowhere near the truth. But carry on."

"I suspected," he said, and then continued. "Every week at Bible class, when it was time for prayer requests from the group, Ken would always ask for the same thing. He would ask that everyone in the room pray for your change of heart, pray you would see that you were wrong to abandon him and that you would come to love him again and let him see his sons."

"Go on, Joe," I said. I could hear him take a deep breath. It was a long, long way from Edmonton to the man in Virginia on the other end of the line, but I felt as though he was sitting right beside me. I could imagine him slowly shaking his head as he told his tale. I knew very well what he was going through: he had trusted and believed, only to have his loyalty rewarded with deception. I had also experienced that moment of the truth dawning and that feeling of having been a fool. But the story wasn't over yet.

"One day, just a short time ago, Ken came to the Bible class very upset. We were all concerned. He was always so stalwart and cheerful. We were shocked to see him so down."

Joe told me that Kenner finally allowed himself to be drawn out by those in the class. He explained that he'd had some very bad news. He had learned that I, in my work as a television journalist, had been involved in the crash of a news helicopter just outside Seattle, Washington. Apparently the pilot and some members of my crew had been killed, but I, miraculously, had survived. In truth, there had recently been reports of a TV station's news helicopter going down near Seattle, with some people on board killed and others hurt. The story had been in the news and so it likely rang a bell with those in the class. For Kenner's purposes, I had been the reporter on board. They couldn't know or understand that I wasn't even working in the US. I was in Canada, in a city that was a long, long way from Seattle.

"The men in the class were shocked," said Joe. "Instead of praying for your change of heart, they were now praying for the Lord to spare your life."

A week later, just before the next Bible class, Kenner asked if he could speak to the group. Joe agreed.

"He stood before us all and talked for an hour on the subject of death," said Joe. "I've never seen anything like it. He spoke about what the Bible says about death. He quoted famous authors and other philosophies. He had the whole class in the palm of his hand. No one said a word. We could barely breathe."

Joe paused. "And then," he said, "he told us he had now been informed that his wife had died."

"The men openly wept for him," Joe said. "But for some reason—I don't know why—I felt that something was wrong."

Joe said he asked Kenner to stay after the class. "I wanted to know how he had been notified of your death. He told me he had a letter from one of your sisters. I asked him whether he'd mind if I saw the letter. 'No problem,' he said. 'Come to my cell tomorrow and you can have it.'"

The next day Joe went and got the letter. "I took it home with me," he said. "I opened it and read it. But what Ken didn't know is that I still had the previous week's letter to you at my house. I hadn't sent it because I didn't know where it should go, what hospital you were in. My wife and I opened the letter he had written to you and the one that was supposed to have come from your sister. We compared the type size and style. We looked for clues in the individual letters on the page. There was no doubt in our minds. The letter to you and the letter he claimed was from your sister had both been written on the same typewriter—the one in Ken's cell."

This wasn't merely a deception, he explained. There was real danger here. After Kenner first told the class I had been critically injured, the news fanned out through the prison. A collection was taken up so that Kenner could afford to send flowers to the hospital. He had accepted their kind donation. Now they had done it again so that he could send more flowers, this time for my funeral. If the prisoners learned they had been deceived, that he had lied to them and manipulated them, they would attack—maybe even kill—him.

"I went to one of the prison administrators right away," said Joe. "He was the first person to call your boss at the TV station, asking if you were alive or dead. I made the second call. We had to know if Kenner was lying. If you were dead, then the story was true. If you were alive, then he had been lying to us. You are obviously alive." Joe let out a long breath.

"I am. And Joe, I'm sorry, but you have been taken in by him. You're not the only one."

"Your turn," he said.

I explained that we had not been married as long as Kenner said and that we certainly did not have two small boys. I worked for CBC Television and could assure him there was no contract or arrangement such as he had described. As for the helicopter crash, although I was a television news reporter, I was a long, long way from the location of that tragedy—not even in the same country. I had never received a single letter or flower. It was all a sham. I outlined the real story for Joe, the truth as far as I knew it. The silence on the other end of the phone was interrupted only briefly by sighs.

Kenner was moved to another prison before his fellow inmates could learn the truth. The mystery of how he had come to be in Leesburg, Virginia, in the first place would be solved for me, but only on my next trip to Britain.

CHAPTER 15

A Journey's End

The cold winter weather had closed in on Edmonton. A chill wind over the prairies swept in light snow and turned the landscape into a hundred shades of grey and white. I was at my desk at CBC Television, my head a thousand miles away as I worked on a story. My telephone rang.

"Hello. Is this Donna?"

That caught me by surprise, as my broadcast name was Lee and hardly anyone even knew Donna was my first name. But things soon became clear. The woman's voice sounded as though it was coming from far away and it carried the familiar melody of a Welsh accent. What now? I wondered.

"Yes. Who is this, please?"

"Oh, Donna, I am so relieved to have reached you," the she continued.

"I'm a nursing sister at the Cottage Hospital in Llandudno. I hope you don't mind me calling you, but there was nothing else that I could do."

199

"Is this about Primrose?" I asked.

"It is, dear," she said. "We have Prim here. I'm afraid I must tell you that she is dying."

I knew this phone call would come one day.

"Donna, we can't reach Kenner. Primrose seems to think he's in jail and won't be able to come to her."

"That's right. He's in prison in the United States."

The sister paused. "Prim is asking for you. She has no one—no one but you. Can you come? She doesn't have much time."

We spoke a moment longer. I hung up the phone and headed for my boss's office. I explained the situation to him and he kindly suggested I take two weeks of my vacation and go.

I landed at Heathrow and headed for Euston Station and the train to North Wales. The London-to-Holyhead was leaving almost immediately. I was aboard. I slept a little, slouched in the seat with my head resting against the window until we pulled into the Bangor station.

Although I was physically tired, it was impossible to truly rest. I kept sifting through my thoughts, trying to sort out what to tell Primrose. I believed in saying the truth, but was she in any condition to hear it? In her final days, would it be a kindness simply to care for her and keep all hurt away? I really didn't know.

I found a hotel room, checked in, collected myself for a few minutes and then went down to the lobby to get a taxi. Soon I was outside the door of the Cottage Hospital in Llandudno. My knock was answered by one of the nursing sisters.

"Donna!" she said. "You're here! Oh, how wonderful. Come in, come in, dear."

"Hello, Sister. How did you know who I was?" I hadn't even spoken and she had already called me by name.

"By your picture, dear," she said. "It's the only one that Primrose brought with her. She keeps it by her bed."

I followed her into a small private room. There was Primrose, propped up with pillows. She seemed so tiny. Her springy grey hair was, as usual, untamed. Her apple cheeks were drained of colour. She looked deflated, defeated.

When she turned to see who was there, her eyes settled on me.

"Donna. Donna." She held out her arms.

Just as I had years earlier when I first walked into her home, I put my arms around her and let her cry.

"I'll dry my tears now," she said after a while. "Thank you for coming. I have no one. No husband, no sister. Not even my son. He should be here, but he's not.

"I'm here," I said. "Now, tell me what I can do to help you and I will."

During my visits over the next few days, Primrose told me what she wanted organized and dealt with. The list was short. Her possessions were few and there was no one to give them to. She tried to persuade me to accept the beautiful set of cups on the top shelf of the china cabinet, but I was afraid they wouldn't survive the journey over-seas intact.

Having some company and extra attention seemed to help Primrose rally. Eventually she recovered enough to go home, but the doctor made it clear that the improvement was likely to be only temporary.

"I know it is," said Primrose, "but I'd rather be at home, even for a few days. I want my own things around me."

So back we went to 11 Glan Peris. The street was quiet. The patch of garden outside the kitchen door was scraggly and overgrown. The house seemed a sad place, but Primrose was relieved to be back in her favourite corner of the living room. I lit the coal fire, made tea and settled her in.

For the rest of my visit she was quiet, circumspect. All the stories of her past had been told. Instead she spoke about her will, and I helped her write it.

Primrose wasn't well enough to leave the house. Social Services arranged for a nurse to visit her each day, and a few faithful friends came to have tea and encourage her. The visits revived their endless pastime of cheeky teasing and habitual complaining, but there was little of the old energy in their banter. When the women were gone, Primrose would grow quiet. She wanted to talk about Kenner and yet she didn't. I walked a fine line, letting her lead the conversation.

"I don't know where I went wrong," she would say. "Where did I make a mistake with him? I tried to give him a good life, but I didn't have much to give." Her eyes would brim with tears. There was nothing much I could tell her.

"Primrose, you did your best. No one can ask more than that." I'd pat her hand, and go and make a pot of tea. That didn't help much other than being a bit of a distraction. Then, with a cup in hand, she'd say whatever was in her heart. I just listened, as I had in the beginning.

The day I was leaving, Primrose held on to me for a long time. "Thank you for coming, Donna." She dissolved into tears. "I know they called you because they thought I was dying right away. But I think I'll be all right now . . . for a bit. Maybe I can get strong enough to go walk in the fields.

That's what I'd really like to do—just take one more walk through the fields."

"I'll be in touch." I gave her a last hug but couldn't let myself look back at the forlorn woman on the couch. I knew her friends would be there shortly, and the nurse, as well, but I felt I was abandoning her. My heart hurt.

I had left Llandudno a bit earlier than necessary because I wanted to give myself enough time to make a quick visit to Uncle Will in Caernarfon before I caught the train to London. I found my way through the narrow streets near the old castle wall and knocked on his door. He lived like a hermit. His lonely life of total blindness revolved around visits by his home help and listening to the radio and a television audio service. I had contacted his social worker to see if it was all right to visit him and she had encouraged me.

When I knocked on the door, I heard him call out *"Dewch i mewn!* Come in!"

"Uncle Will, it's Donna. I've come to visit you."

"Oh, Donna!" He was clearly pleased. "My social worker told me you were here helping Prim. Oh, come in, come in."

Uncle Will appeared in the corner, emerging from the kitchen. His three-room flat was dark and dingy. The air was stale, musty and old. His world was dark anyway, so no curtains were open to let in the sun. Only one light was on. Uncle Will was thinner, frailer than when I had seen him just a few years earlier when he and Primrose had come to Winchmore Hill for Christmas. He looked as though he was fading away. The elbows on his suit were worn thin, the cuffs frayed. His knitted waistcoat was missing a few buttons. I gave him a brief hug and we sat down to chat.

"Donna—now, tell me . . . tell me, girl. What is going on with that nephew of mine? Why isn't he here taking care of Prim? There's talk around the town that he's in jail again. Is he?"

I drew a deep breath. I felt I owed Uncle Will the truth. I told him about what had happened to me. I told him about Kenner being in prison in the US. As the details came out, however sparsely, Uncle Will collapsed more deeply into his soft chair.

His expression alternated between shock and anger. When I told him how hurt I was, how heartbroken, Uncle Will began to cry.

"Excuse me," he said. He fished a creased, grimy handkerchief from his pocket and wiped his eyes. "I am so, so sorry," he whispered.

"For what, Uncle Will?" I said. "None of this is your fault."

"Oh, but it is, it is," he said. "I could have warned you about him, but I didn't. I knew he was a bad one. He's always been a bad one. But you were so happy and I felt maybe now, maybe this time, he would go straight. Maybe his love for you would make him turn his life around." He paused and sighed and wiped his eyes again. "I am still head of this family," he said. "He is my responsibility and I have let everyone down."

It hurt to see him like this. He was trying to take responsibility in an Old World kind of way.

"No, Uncle Will," I argued as gently and firmly as I could. "No one holds you responsible. I certainly don't."

"But I am, my dear girl, I am. I knew and I didn't warn you. The last time he came here," said Uncle Will, "he made like he was my loving nephew. He prepared the tea. We chatted. He told me all kinds of wonderful things about how he was married now and deserved some support in starting a new life. I was happy for him. But then he told me that I should give him money. I told him to forget it. I don't have extra money. I'm a pensioner."

Uncle Will paused and looked off into the distance with eyes that could see nothing. "He was angry with me, and we didn't part on very good terms. After he left, I slammed the door. But then I had a thought.

"I went to my cabinet, to my secret spot where I keep my money. It had all gone. It was there before he came because I had checked it. After he had left, it was all gone. He stole from his old, blind uncle."

Uncle Will dissolved into muttering in Welsh. I couldn't really follow or understand him. I hugged him again and said goodbye, my heart heavy.

Sitting on the train, heading back to London, I tried to sift through my conflicting feelings about what I had said to Uncle Will, because sharing the truth also meant sharing the misery. What good had it done, really, to bring the stories about Kenner through Uncle Will's door? I wasn't sure. Just because it happened, was it really necessary to tell him? Was it kind? I had upset him and left him blaming himself for feeling powerless to help me or to prevent Kenner from doing it all again. I wanted to leave him feeling better for my visit. I left him feeling worse.

I didn't see him again.

I'm so sorry, Uncle Will.

CHAPTER 16

Meeting with Mary

B efore flying back to Canada, I travelled from North Wales to Walton-on-Thames in Surrey for a meeting I had arranged on the phone with Mary. Her barrage of letters had suddenly stopped after Kenner had left her home to relocate to the US.

I was thankful to be able to think about it all in the peaceful isolation of the railway carriage as the train rolled slowly through towns and the countryside on its way to London. At Waterloo Station I boarded the same train I had taken only a few years earlier when Kenner had brought me to Walton-on-Thames and formally proposed.

A taxi delivered me to Mary's house. The door opened before I could knock.

"Donna."

"Hello, Mary."

She was very much as I had imagined her. A trim woman of medium height, she appeared to be in her late sixties. Her grey hair was brushed back in waves. She wore no makeup or jewellery. She looked intelligent and sensible. We took a moment to smile at each other. I followed her through the house and into a beautiful room with white lace curtains pulled back from the windows to offer a view of the garden. There were two softly upholstered wing-back chairs, and a polished, low table with tea and biscuits laid out. We settled ourselves. As I still wasn't sure what I was going to hear, I let her lead the conversation.

"Please," she said, "let me begin by offering you my apologies. There I was, having the audacity to chastise and advise you, and all the while Kenner was telling me a pack of lies. I was a fool."

For the next few hours we sipped tea and compared our stories. As the saying goes, misery loves company. We each found ourselves outraged and relieved. The outrage flared easily as we each explained the intricate, unending manipulations and frauds Kenner had perpetrated. There was some consolation in knowing we weren't alone in falling victim to Kenner's charming plausibility, his convincing portrayal of sincerity and heartbreak.

I scribbled down as completely as I could everything Mary said. Kenner had told her that he and I had a son named Richard, who was at boarding school in Victoria, Canada. He further explained that I had contracted some dreadful disease as a reporter doing a story on drug abuse. This disease had left me paralyzed from the waist down. With his tale of my critical illness and the need for boarding school fees for "Richard," Kenner obtained the sympathy of some wealthy person in Walton-on-Thames, who gave him money for my "treatment" and "Richard's school fees."

Somehow Kenner had managed to buy himself a Mercedes and have it shipped to the US. Mary believes the money he used for that was supposed to come to me—likely the money loaned to him for my "treatment." Mary said she could never understand why he insisted on staying in the UK when I was ill, indeed half paralyzed, leaving a lonely son in boarding school.

Kenner also managed to get a bank card from a fellow boarder at Mary's house, as well as a bank withdrawal document. Shortly before he left Britain, Kenner emptied the man's account, taking every single pound. Throughout his stay with Mary, instead of hiding his actions, Kenner had seemed to flirt with the danger of being discovered. He arranged for people he knew to meet, compare stories and possibly find him out. He brought Primrose down to Walton-on-Thames, where she stayed for a week. Of course Primrose and Mary talked, exposing some obvious contradictions.

Kenner showed Mary a letter allegedly from Stanford University saying he had been awarded a PhD. (In our time together he had offered a similar story. He produced a letter he claimed was from a university in Montreal. The doctorate he said they conferred on him was for some spectacular work in economics.)

Mary described Kenner's dramatics when he claimed he had just received an employment contract with a publisher to write articles for a magazine. He came home with it typed on company letterhead, and put on quite a show for Mary and Kathleen. He was overjoyed, dancing about and clapping gleefully. Mary had been so pleased. She added that shortly thereafter, with his new and abundant income, he showered the two women with attention on Mother's

Day. While she enjoyed the food and gifts, she felt uncomfortable, as Kenner completely ignored his own mother. In spite of Mary's urging he made no effort in that regard, and Primrose was left alone and unappreciated.

Mary had been disconcerted by Kenner's behaviour in church. She described his forced, overloud, overemphasized responses and prayers, and his pious, straight-backed posture with hands perfectly folded. She also said there were two or three times when Kenner—in her words—"looked evil." One time was when he gave her a phony account of his personal history. Another time was in church. She said his face looked its most terrible at the "exchanging of the peace" in the church service. She hid her own face so others in the congregation wouldn't see how shocked she was. I told her I knew that face.

One story in particular cleared up a question I had been unable to answer: When Kenner relocated to the US, why did he choose Leesburg, Virginia?

Kenner had told Mary with great excitement that he had been hired to work as a journalist in the US. She wasn't certain if it was for the BBC or the CBC. It didn't seem to matter, because in his usual persuasive manner, he made Mary believe he was headed for advancement and adventure.

"The day he left," she said, "he drove away in the Mercedes. I remember the car was filled with electronics of various sorts—radios and some kind of sound equipment. And things I didn't recognize. I'm not sure what that was all about, but I didn't think too much of it at the time." She paused. "I see now that this was a problem of mine: I didn't pay proper attention."

After he left, the debris began to float to the surface. She realized that behind her back her had secretly drained her bank account. Kenner had also tried to extract money by creating financial charges against Mary and Kathleen's property. She now felt she was in some danger of losing her home. "Kathleen was suspicious of him right from the start," she said. "She tried to warn me, but I wouldn't listen."

Then a letter arrived, addressed to Kenner.

"Now, I would never, ever open another person's mail," she said. "But I was now aware that I had been dealing with a skilled con artist. And when I looked at the envelope, the handwriting seemed to be that of an elderly lady. I just didn't feel right about what might be happening, so I opened it. Inside was a letter from a woman in Leesburg, Virginia.

Ah, I thought—here we go.

Mary explained that the woman had written saying she just happened to think of Kenner again and wanted to thank him for his kindness a short while ago at Heathrow Airport.

Mary still had the letter, and referred to it as she told me the story: "'I hope you remember me, Mr. Jones. I had just come in on a flight from France and was struggling with my luggage,'"

Kenner had appeared just in time to help a lady in distress. Once on the scene, he lent cheerful assistance. He handled her baggage, made sure she had a cup of tea and a bit of a rest and then got her safely into a taxi.

Mary continued: "She wrote that the last thing she remembered of Kenner was his smiling face as he waved goodbye when the taxi pulled away. He had left his business card with her. Now she felt she simply must write and tell him how much she had appreciated his help." The woman from Leesburg closed her letter by adding that if she could ever repay his kindness, she would.

It seemed clear, knowing Kenner as we felt we did, that this was a well-planned scheme. How many times had he waited at an airport for the right person to come along? And there she was—an elderly woman, well dressed, travelling alone, needing a helping hand. In the midst of her confusion, a charming man appears and he makes everything go smoothly. They exchange a limited amount of personal information in the brief time they are together. He learns her name and where she lives. He, in a gentlemanly fashion, leaves her with his card.

How perfect, then, if he just happens to be in Leesburg, Virginia. How perfect if he happens to encounter her again, in a restaurant, walking in the park, shopping. How perfect for her to have a chance to repay his kindness by welcoming him into her home, befriending him, introducing him to her circle of friends. Yes. Leesburg, Virginia, would be the perfect place.

But Mary intervened. She found a telephone number for the woman and placed a call to warn her about Kenner.

"She was shocked," Mary said. "She appreciated hearing from me and felt she'd likely had a narrow escape. She said she would be careful to stay as far away from Kenner as she could."

A short time later the same woman sent Mary an envelope with newspaper clippings. The stories told how Kenner had gone into the offices of the local newspaper and asked for a job. Mary handed the clippings to me while recounting what had happened.

"The newspaper editor said Kenner came in all tweedy looking, walking with a cane. He won over the staff by seeming to be a good reporter whose primary interest wasn't money but, rather, 'getting a feel for local politics.' They said he was charming, interesting and highly intelligent."

Mary and I just looked at each other.

"And then the inevitable happened. Frauds, forged cheques. He was eventually indicted by a grand jury. Bail had been set at $25,000—and somehow obtained."

At this point I could now take up the story. I told Mary about the call from Joe, the visitor counsellor at Virginia State Prison who had telephoned my place of work to ask if I was alive or dead. She sat gently shaking her head.

Our stories shared, we parted perhaps wiser about the details but both still feeling baffled and embarrassed at our gullibility. It was comforting, in a way, to have met another person who had fallen for Kenner's game. It was not, however, enough to erase the self-questioning for having missed all the signs and signals. We took our inner questions away from the meeting, both of us pleased we had met, but neither of us with any real answers.

CHAPTER 17

Listen to Me

B ack in Edmonton a few weeks later, I received a phone call from one of Primrose's neighbours. Primrose had suddenly taken a turn for the worse. Her heart finally failed her. She was gone.

She had been holding out a dim hope to the end that Kenner would somehow come to her side.

But he was still behind bars in Virginia State Prison.

When Kenner was eventually paroled he wasted no time in breaking the conditions of his release. He crossed the border into Canada and travelled from Ontario back to British Columbia, defrauding, leaving a trail of financial debris behind him.

Although I was still in Edmonton, Alberta, I was contacted by police in the Vancouver area. Kenner was still referring to me either as his wife or as a contact. I was always easy to find.

Although I wanted to go home to the west coast, I hesitated to do so because Kenner was there. The Rocky Mountains that separate British Columbia and Alberta were like a barricade of safety for me. Eventually I saw that I was allowing my fear to rule my decisions. I found a job at a television station in Victoria, on Vancouver Island, packed my bags and headed for home territory.

I had some vague information about Kenner's whereabouts and managed to get a phone number for him. I felt I needed to face him and establish my boundaries.

We spoke for the first time in years. It was a brief conversation. I said I wanted to see him and suggested the lobby of the Hotel Vancouver the next day at 10:00 a.m. He agreed.

I took the first ferry from the island to the Lower Mainland and downtown Vancouver. I had chosen the Hotel Vancouver because I wanted to be somewhere visible and public in case of trouble. By mid-morning I was walking through the lobby of the hotel, but I kept going and found a quiet, remote part of the hotel café, out of sight. I sat there until just after the appointed meeting time and then walked to the main lobby. Kenner was there.

We shook hands briefly, which seemed very strange somehow. The divorce had already gone through and I was no longer Mrs. Kenner Elias Jones. I steeled myself, ready for the inevitable wave of charm. We sat down in a couple of soft chairs in a quiet corner.

"You look wonderful, Don," said Kenner.

He hadn't changed. He was wearing a dark suit, crisp white shirt and silk tie. Shoes polished. Hands manicured. It was spooky to be sitting there across from him.

"I've come to tell you a few things," I began.

Kenner seemed willing to listen. I would like to be able to say that I was calm and in complete control of my emotions. That is not the truth. Inside I was in turmoil, even though I had thought through carefully what I wanted to say and how I was going to say it. My message was going to be simple and direct.

I was not smiling.

"Don't be cold with me, Don."

Kenner was taking his best shot at deciding the tone of the meeting.

I was having none of it.

"I have some things to say to you, Kenner, which are best said face to face."

He waited, his face composed as if he were a clergyman. I carried on.

"This won't take long. I want to begin by thanking you for all the good things that happened while we were together."

That caught him off guard. I didn't pause.

"We had some wonderful times and I had a chance to live in Britain. I learned many things. You were great company, mostly. I'm sorry that's not all that happened, but thank you for the good things."

He was silent. This for sure wasn't what he had expected me to say. But I wasn't finished.

"And now I'm going to tell you the rest."

To his credit, he didn't get up and leave. I forged ahead, keeping my tone as even as possible.

"Kenner, you dragged me through hell. All the lying, the money troubles, making me believe that James was coming to kill us. No. No, don't interrupt me, please."

He had obviously wanted to comment, but I held up my hand, indicating he should stop.

"I was very, very close to having an emotional break-down. My life in the six years since we parted has been spent paying off your debts, dealing with the consequences of things I did not do, that you got me tangled up in, and I'm not out of it yet. I have lost friends over all of this. I have had family members doubt me and think that surely I must have been aware of what you were doing."

"Don, I . . ."

He leaned forward to claim the conversation. I shook my head. "No. Please. I insist you let me finish."

He sat back in his chair again, hands folded perfectly in his lap. The clergyman face returned.

"Even recently, I have been contacted by people who have heard about me through you, and again by the police."

I took a deep breath, to settle myself before saying the next thing on my mind.

"There is something you don't know."

I could feel the tears wanting to spring into my eyes, but I fought them back.

"You and I had a baby."

The well-composed face across from me changed. He wasn't expecting this, either.

"What?" was all he could say.

"When I was coming home on St. David's Day and you met me drunk at the station, I was thinking all the way home about when to tell you. Yes, I was pregnant, Kenner."

He looked shocked. It was the only time I had seen that in his face.

"And that night, with your terrible letter and the stress

of believing that James was on the rampage and we were in huge danger, I lost the baby. I lost her, and I have carried the grief of that ever since. I didn't tell you at the time because what was the point? You were—we were—struggling with all the fallout from the things you had done. I have lived with the loss of my baby ever since. But the fault was yours. *You* live with that."

He sat very still. The complete composure with which he had begun was thin enough to see through.

I leaned forward. "Now, you listen to me. I have already been to the police in Vancouver and in Victoria, and I have been to my lawyer. Everyone knows you are here and knows the real story. If you ever, ever, ever mention my name again or write my name on a piece of paper, I will know and I will have the law down on you so fast it will make your head spin. Now—you stay away from me."

I quietly got up and left him sitting there.

CHAPTER 18

-- -- -- -- --

Burden of Proof

My meeting with Kenner had the desired effect in that I stopped hearing from people who had encountered him and believed I was part of whatever deception was underway. But my involvement in his world wasn't over yet. The justice system once again caught up with Kenner and put him in Oakalla prison in Burnaby, British Columbia.

He wasn't idle. He filled some of his time by writing about life behind bars, and had an article published in a Vancouver newspaper. In it he outlined the difficulties of coping with not only being in prison but being in one that was old and in poor repair. He finished his story by borrowing from Shakespeare, saying he would end his day "and sleep, perchance to dream."

An elderly widow named Elsie Hager read the articles and apparently was enchanted. She decided she absolutely had to meet the man who wrote them. She went to visit Kenner in Oakalla and a close friendship developed. Once he was released, Elsie, more than thirty-five years his senior, welcomed him into her home. Eventually they married.

Elsie was functionally blind. Kenner helped her with church work, gave sermons at services in her church, wrote promotional material for her, sang in the choir and organized a youth club. He looked after the household, drove her to her appointments and read to her.

I first learned about Elsie's connection to Kenner through a radio news story. I was driving through Victoria one day, heading for work at the television station. The broadcast included a story on what appeared to be a hostage-taking and extortion attempt in Greater Vancouver. A victim named Kenner Jones had dropped off his passenger, Elsie Hager, at the home they shared and then gone to park her car. When an unusual amount of time passed and he didn't return, she became alarmed. More time passed and then her telephone rang. A man told her he had kidnapped Kenner and was holding him and her vehicle for ransom. Elsie was instructed to prepare a payment of thousands of dollars. She was apprised where to drop it off the next day—a Vancouver address—and directed not to contact police or there would be dire consequences.

According to the newscast, Elsie hung up and immediately called the police. They attended, wrote down the information and next morning staked out the location where Elsie had been advised to drop off the money. They captured the perpetrator and took Kenner Jones safely to the station to provide a statement.

The moment I arrived at work I contacted the radio station's newsroom and identified myself. I urged them to research Kenner Jones. They needed to satisfy themselves they were on firm ground with the story. It was dropped from their next newscast.

I also telephoned the Royal Canadian Mounted Police. I reached the lead investigator on the file, explained who I was and asked to see him. I told him I had information that I felt he had to see. He was less than enthusiastic about giving me any time. I had the feeling my position as a television newscaster was the only reason he agreed to see me at all.

The next day I travelled from Vancouver Island to the Lower Mainland by ferry. At the RCMP detachment I was shown into the investigator's office. I was carrying a thick file in my hand. The officer made it clear by his body language and cold courtesy that he wasn't much interested in my visit. As I sat down, he didn't even sit squarely to the desk. Instead he turned to the side as if he really couldn't be bothered.

I began. I gave him a brief summary of my involvement with Kenner. When he realized I was an ex-wife, his face registered even more skepticism. I could almost read his thought: Woman with a grudge. But his attitude began to thaw as I went through my file. Page by page I placed on the desk in front of him Kenner's various records. I had newspaper articles. I had copies of the forged cheques and documents from London and elsewhere.

He picked up the first page in a lackadaisical fashion. But then with the second, he turned in his chair to sit facing me. By the third page his elbows were on the desk as he read. The skepticism vanished, replaced by surprise. At the end of my presentation he put the papers down and looked at me.

"I took Kenner's statement," he said. "In fact, he wrote it out for me in longhand."

The officer opened his own file and withdrew a stack of paper. There was Kenner's familiar handwriting.

The officer summarized the circumstances for me, as they had been described to him. Kenner had been kidnapped. Elsie had been phoned and an extortion demand made. But when the police hid at the ransom drop location, they saw Kenner and the alleged kidnapper sharing cigarettes and walking back and forth, talking and laughing. Police were baffled because there had been plenty of time and opportunity for Kenner to make a getaway, to run for safety. But he hadn't.

"When I challenged him on that," the RCMP officer explained, "Kenner said he was afraid that if he made a run for it, the bad guy would go after Elsie and hurt her, so he stayed put. And I believed him.

"I've been in this kind of work for twenty-five years," he said. "It's my job to know when I'm being lied to. And I didn't know."

He paused and looked at me. "He's good. He's really good."

The officer took copies of my documents then saw me out with a handshake and words of genuine appreciation for my visit.

I never knew the outcome of the file, but I seem to recall hearing that the case died on the vine because Kenner wouldn't testify against the alleged extortionist. If Elsie ever learned the truth of the apparently fake ransom caper, it didn't seem to matter. She either forgave him or believed his version of the story, whatever that might have been. It seems there was nothing Kenner could do that would motivate Elsie to send him away.

In the meantime, the Canadian Immigration authorities had been working on their Kenner Elias Jones file, with the intent of getting him out of the country, never to return. True to his word, Bill's efforts from the Immigration office in Nanaimo had been successful. His report to his superiors was strong enough to persuade them to revoke Kenner's Landed Immigrant status and remove him from Canada.

When he was served with the deportation order, Kenner had a choice: leave Canada or appeal the order. Kenner decided to fight. Somehow he had the funds necessary to hire a lawyer considered one of the best. A hearing date was set for Kenner's appeal. His task and that of his lawyer was to persuade a court that he deserved to stay in Canada.

My experiences and information were going to be a significant part of the case against Kenner. In preparation for my testimony, I received a large file from the office of a lawyer in Citizenship and Immigration Canada. We spoke a few times on the phone and met briefly the day before the hearing. I was advised that the largest block of time was set aside for me.

The hearing would take place in a courtroom and would in almost every way be like a trial. Instead of a single judge, though, three people would sit as a tribunal. There would be two lawyers, one for the appellant, Kenner, and one for Immigration Canada. Spectators were allowed in. Testimony would be recorded, just as it was in a regular court of law.

When I arrived, I was told to sit in a waiting room set aside for witnesses until they were called into the courtroom. As I came through the door, I could see Kenner and an elderly woman on the far side. This clearly was Elsie, his new partner. I chose a corner seat as far from them as possible.

It was quite a scene. Elsie was seated comfortably. She was stout and matronly, with grey hair and glasses. She looked to be in her mid-seventies. She and Kenner seemed to be a bizarre mismatch. I admit I felt strangely relieved, somehow, that she was so different from me.

But I was soon distracted from my musings by curious theatre on the other side of the room.

Kenner was hovering near Elsie, talking with her and patting her hand. A coterie of people, mostly women, were fluttering around her, bringing tea, wrapping a shawl around her and placing soothing hands on her shoulders. Elsie sat imperious, like a queen surrounded by her court.

Eventually Kenner noticed me. I had started reading a newspaper, but out of the corner of my eye I could see him approaching. I took a deep breath.

"Don."

He strode toward me, rubbing his hands together in that characteristic washing motion. His head was tilted slightly. He was smiling. He made as if wanting to shake my hand, but I did not release the newspaper, only lowered it.

"Hello." I had nothing more to say.

But Kenner did.

"I wanted to thank you for all you did for Mother."

Ah. I had wondered what his opening comment would be. However, I was not even remotely interested in being drawn into a conversation.

"Don't thank me, Kenner," I said. "I didn't do it for you. I did it for her."

He wasn't sure how to respond to that and I wasn't going to help him out of the awkward moment.

"Well," he said finally, "thank you anyway."

He gathered himself as if everything was going exactly as he desired, turned and walked back to Elsie.

Before long someone came into the room and announced that the hearing was beginning. Kenner left to take his place in the courtroom. The contingent of supporters also left to find seats.

Now only three of us remained in the waiting room. One, a person I didn't know, apparently had a short testimony to give. Then the court was going to call Elsie. The Immigration lawyer had told me Elsie would be on the witness stand just before me but wasn't going to be there for long, either.

The unknown person was called into court. That left Elsie and me alone. I kept my newspaper in front of my face. Suddenly Elsie broke the silence.

"He still loves *you*."

Her voice carried a sob mixed with anger. I would have been surprised to hear her speak to me at all but certainly hadn't expected to hear those words—and in that tone.

I lowered the corner of the paper and looked over at her.

"Do not speak to me," I said.

"No!" she said. "You have to hear this! You're still the *only* woman in the world for him. He still loves *you*."

This sounded like something straight out of high school, something an adolescent would say to a rival who was getting all the attention. I had to stomp this out right away.

"I said, *Don't speak to me*. If you insist on talking to me, I will go and get security. I don't have to listen to you."

She was clearly perturbed, harrumphing and sighing. I continued to hide behind my newspaper until I was rescued from more of Elsie's laments when a couple of her companions fluttered in to say she was now required in the courtroom. They adjusted her shawl, made sure she had her cane and supported her on either side. The parade shuffled along. As Elsie passed by, the air was infused with the smell of aging skin, tired shoes and soap.

It wasn't long before one of the court staff came to fetch me. I walked through the double doors, up the aisle and onto the witness stand. The Immigration lawyer had warned me of two things. He said Kenner and his lawyer would be sitting close to the witness stand. This was true. Kenner was just out of arm's reach. I resolved to pay no attention to his expressions or body language as I testified. I was also told about Kenner's lawyer—that he had a reputation for being sharp, combative, and ruthless, and would try to upset me and catch me off guard. After being sworn in, I settled myself as best I could. The long day of questioning was under way.

I don't remember exactly what set her off, but at one point I said something that brought Elsie to her feet.

"She's a snake! She's lying!" Elsie's shouting filled the courtroom from the back, where she had been sitting. "Don't believe her!"

"Quiet, please." The judge acting as the chair of the tribunal banged a gavel. "Please continue," he said to me.

I picked up where I had left off. But whatever I was describing was more than Elsie could bear. She was on her feet again, shouting.

"She's lying! She's a snake in the grass! Don't listen to her! She's—"

The gavel slammed again. This time with more force.

"Silence. If you can't control yourself, madam, I will have you removed."

By now Elsie's entourage was fanning her, cooing, patting and encouraging her to sit. More than one acid glance came my way. It was difficult not to laugh.

When all was quiet again, my testimony continued. I eventually managed to irritate Kenner's lawyer, as well. During cross-examination he tried badgering me by using a hectoring tone, scornful expressions and interrupting me when I was trying to respond to his question or challenge. I knew he was baiting me and I decided to toss some attitude back at him.

"Hey," I said sharply after a curt and rude onslaught from him, "why don't you let me finish?"

Looking wounded, hands out, palms up, he applied for sympathy from the tribunal. "Your Honour!" He was calling on the presiding judge to reprimand me. The judge turned to me with a look of *behave yourself* everywhere on his face but in his eyes. I didn't wait.

"Your Honour," I pleaded. "He keeps asking me questions and then interrupts and turns his back on me. If he'd shut up long enough to let me finish, he would have his answers."

The judge was struggling not to smile. "Well, perhaps both parties could exercise patience," he said.

The admonishment had little effect on Kenner's fractious advocate, but he did give me slightly more time to respond.

During our lunch break the Immigration lawyer said he was pleased with how everything was going but there was no way to guess how the tribunal would rule. If they decided in favour of Kenner, he would retain his Landed Immigrant status and could stay in Canada as long as he wanted. If they decided against him, then the deportation order would be upheld and he would be required to leave, given a date to depart and put on a flight out of the country.

Through the remainder of the day Elsie managed to keep herself in check. It was apparently more important to stay in the courtroom and listen than to accuse me of being in league with the devil. The hearing ended and we were all dismissed. Kenner, Elsie and the entourage swept from the courtroom en masse then vanished down the hallway.

It took a few months before the tribunal produced a long document carefully and completely outlining the evidence that had been brought before them and the decision it had led them to. After dozens of pages it was really just the final remarks that mattered:

> The onus of proof is on the appellant (Kenner
> Elias Jones) to establish that he should not be
> removed from Canada. In this case, the appellant
> has not met the burden of proof. The Appeal

Division is of the opinion that the risk to Canadian Society, given his past criminal history and the lack of compelling evidence of rehabilitation, is too great.

Accordingly, based on all the evidence before it, the Appeal Division finds that the deportation order is valid in law and further finds, having regard to all the circumstances of the case, the appellant has not satisfied it that he should not be removed from Canada. Accordingly, the appeal is dismissed.

The order was dated May 3, 1991. Kenner had lost. He was served again with a deportation order and told to present himself at Vancouver Airport at a certain date and time.

He and Elsie did not appear. They had already moved to California.

Immigration Canada didn't really care. He was out of the country and barred from coming back.

That sounded good to me.

CHAPTER 19

Time to Tell All

After Kenner left Canada and I was on my own, I tried to find my way to level ground again. It felt good to work and have control of my own finances, even though there were many demands on my earnings. I established a budget for myself and began paying off the mountain of debt that had accumulated behind my back through Kenner's deceptions. Ultimately it took me the better part of ten years to pay it all off. Working at CBC Edmonton was steady, challenging and enjoyable. I had a chance to reinvent myself and start again, and I was grateful for it.

I had allowed myself a bit of money for discretionary spending, and after a while I splurged and bought myself a small computer. How daring I felt. The newsroom was still using manual typewriters. Few people had a computer at home. I cleared the desk in my apartment, making space for a brand new IBM PC Junior and a dot matrix printer. Setting everything up then trying to understand computer instructions that might as well have been a foreign language was an exercise in extreme patience. The floppy disks, the whirring and the random-seeming counterintuitive commands almost defeated me. But I persevered because this computer—"Junior," as I called it—had a job to do. I wanted to write a book.

In the few times I had related the Kenner Jones saga, I had heard the same suggestion: you should write all this down. Looking back, I know in those early days after the experiences that I was just not ready. Everything was all too close and I was too raw. But I didn't really understand that yet. Instead I installed Junior and positioned my hands over the keyboard. I took a deep breath. Junior hummed quietly, waiting to take everything in.

Primrose's stories were fresh and complete in my memory. Writing that part was easy. Then I came to the point in the narrative where I appeared—my backpacking visit to Britain and my first encounter with Kenner. The storytelling was still fairly neutral; after all, it was a bit like writing a travelogue. The tale flew through my fingertips and onto Junior's memory disks.

But when I got to the letters we exchanged, the proposal and where my heart took over from my head, I ran into problems. I was still very angry, embarrassed and emotionally bruised. I realized I wanted to write the story to explain my side. I wanted to justify my foolishness. I wanted to apologize to myself. The most painful parts of the story were just a page or two away. I couldn't go there yet. I put the project aside.

With a few keystrokes Junior sent the eighty pages I had written to the little printer, which *ticka-tick-ticka'd* along, tapping out my words line by line. When the printer was finished, I tore the sheets of fanfold paper apart and put them in an envelope. The envelope went into a box with all the documents, letters, photographs and memories. Just before I put the lid on the box, I looked around for anything else that should go inside. In my desk drawer was Kenner's gold fountain pen. When Kenner left Canada the day Mum and I drove him to the airport, he forgot to take it with him. I picked it up and had a long look at its elegant craftsmanship. Then I placed it in the bottom of the box and closed the lid.

Decades passed. Life carried both Kenner and me farther and farther away from each other. As the years went by, I relaxed and went long periods without hearing or thinking about him. Once in a while a story or an experience would remind me of things that had happened in those tumultuous days. Mostly, though, he was pushed to the back of my memory.

On a storage shelf in the basement the box with the initials KEJ on the side had also been pushed to the back. It was a bit grimy, the corners crumpled with wear and tear. Over the years I had carried that box from place to place, home to home, not wanting to destroy it but also not wanting to open it and let the past out.

One day in 2014 I was rearranging the storage area, when I came across the box. I took it out and put it on a nearby table, realizing that it had been thirty years since Kenner and I had divorced. I lifted the lid and looked inside. The box contained mostly file folders, neatly labelled. There were a few photograph albums and a stack of loose pictures. I picked them up and walked over to the light. There she was. Primrose. Primrose on her wedding day. Primrose in her soft dress. Primrose with her gentle smile and all that uncertainty in her eyes.

The memories returned, but this time they didn't bring pain. I inspected the contents of the box more closely. At the bottom I found the gold fountain pen. I picked it up, admired it and balanced it in my hand.

My disastrous experiences with Kenner had forced me to re-examine how I'd been living my life and what priority I'd been placing on my own happiness. I now looked again at the young woman I'd once been.

In recent years my living space has included a small art studio, a place of creativity, fun and magic. It's a quiet world in which whatever I think or imagine, whatever my impulse is, I am allowed to follow it. With Kenner's gold pen in my hand, I walked into my studio, where the brushes are laid out and the tubes of paint are piled nearby. A fresh canvas was waiting on the easel. I sat down.

For the first time in decades I let myself go back and recall that time of love, dreams and hope. From the safety of my studio chair I also allowed myself to remember the hurt. It was as if taking the lid off the storage box had released everything into the light and there was no turning away.

I'd been young, free-spirited and impressionable when I'd walked down the seaside promenade in Llandudno and signed my name in the tourist office visitors' book using Kenner's pen. Now in my studio I took a deep breath, put the pen down and picked up a brush. My mind's eye was seeing the graceful sweep of Llandudno's beach, the squeeze of hotels, the gentle, rolling waves and the tourists rambling by. It was all very easy to recall. My brush began to move with broad strokes at first, putting vague images onto the clean, white space.

As I worked, I realized that having pushed my memories away for so long, they had become like old photographs with blurry edges and faded colour, but now, with time having done its healing work, the Llandudno promenade in my thoughts started to look new again.

It really is a lovely place. The bracing breeze from the sea casts a freshness over everything. The hotels and cafés shine in the summer sun. The seagulls wheel and cry. Passersby stroll along chatting, laughing and holding hands. How easy it now seemed to celebrate that beautiful town, which for so long I had only regarded as a sad place because it symbolized the beginning of my time with Kenner. My brush tried to keep up with my thoughts as it slid along the canvas.

The young woman in the painting is carrying more than her large orange backpack. She's making a journey while laden with dreams and inexperience. She doesn't know how to use discernment and how to put happiness and safety first. She only knows how to give everything away. I take a finer brush in hand and work on some details. I think about her heart. I think about how vulnerable she was. I want to show understanding where before I felt only anger and embarrassment.

As she walks at a measured pace toward the unknown, there is someone waiting for her in that tourist hut. He will soon be spinning his web and she will be caught. But here, decades later, she sits calmly in her studio, brush in hand. After being afraid to look down those corridors into the past, afraid that I would judge myself and everyone else in the story with harshness, I realize that I am at peace. My journey has brought me back to happiness, love and trust. It has also taught me to rely ultimately upon myself. I am now the one wielding the pen.

After taking a long look at my progress for the day, I wanted to keep going, but not in the studio. My mind moved from the image on the canvas to a photograph I had found in the storage box earlier that day—the one of Primrose in her blue wedding dress.

I left the studio, went to my desk, powered up my computer and opened a new document page. I laughed quietly to myself, thinking this computer is very different from Junior.

And so, with my self, my memories and Prim in my mind and heart, I began to write.

EPILOGUE

\- \- \- \- \- \- \- \- \-

A fter I completed the story of my life with Kenner, as now laid out in pages of this book, I knew from online searches that he had not changed his ways and was still on the run from justice. In the wake of his deportation from Canada he was deemed "a danger to society" in the United States and kicked out. A senior US Immigration officer described him as "the best con man I have ever encountered in my entire career."

Once Kenner was back in Britain after being deported from the US, his theft and fraud offences continued to mount and he chalked up more convictions. From what I could discover, the total counts against him, both before and after our time as husband and wife, is near sixty.

In the south of England in 2003 he was charged with stealing thousands of pounds from an employer. Before facing trial at Lewes Crown Court in East Sussex, he fled. A warrant was immediately issued for his arrest, but he has not been seen in Britain since.

He turned up in Kenya and spent seven years there posing as both a medical doctor and a priest. During this time, he set up a charity—Luke's Fund—and married his third wife, a Kenyan woman, Florence Buyela. Some say his organization was bogus; some say he did good works. In 2010 he abandoned Kenya, his charity and his wife and disappeared, leaving behind debts said to be more than $100,000.

The following year he spent time in Portugal before moving to Spain, all the while endearing himself to people and at the same time defrauding them. Claiming to be a refugee in 2013, he sought asylum in Sweden. Police received reports of him allegedly trying to scam or defraud people, of again attempting to pass himself off as a medical doctor.

Although the Sussex Police still had an active warrant for his arrest, the police in Sweden, as in Portugal and Spain, were unable to effect Kenner's extradition because no European Arrest Warrant had been issued. The Sussex Police invited anyone with information about Kenner to contact them. Some people did, but to no avail—he simply remained at large as a prolific and apparently carefree criminal.

When writing this book, I decided to try to track Kenner down. I was willing to give him the chance to explain his bizarre behaviour and the harm he had caused to so many people. I was not going to offer him a platform to carry on lying and making excuses. I wanted to give him the opportunity to come clean, to tell the truth and express remorse. Would he take it? Would he seek redemption?

But as so many things go in life, the plans we make and

the realities we face can be two different things. Just as I was looking for a way to contact Kenner, hundreds of thousands of desperate Syrians began seeking refuge in Sweden, Kenner's last known hunting ground. I realized I had no hope of locating him on my own.

Still, as with every chapter of this con man's story—just when you think it's over—it's not.

ACKNOWLEDGEMENTS

W ith deep appreciation, I mention some of those who have supported and encouraged me in the writing of this book.

My husband, Harv Allison, has been stalwart, and a source of stable thinking and advice.

My family: Donna Caillet, Maureen Pietrzykowski, Jacki Aubertin, and Fred Bell have been all that I could have wanted, always encouraging and urging me to do my best.

The entire project would not have even begun without Len Port, a "semi-retired" print journalist with worldwide experience, now living in Portugal's Algarve. Discovering him and his online blog with Kenner as a subject led to a dialogue. The dialogue led to me forwarding Len my earliest pages which I had written in the 1980s. Len's reaction to those pages led to him challenging me to write my own story. I love a challenge.

Len accepted my challenge in return, agreeing to do the early editing and organizing of the manuscript. His gentle, firm professionalism was the perfect touch for me.

Friends of Len's, whom I have never met, Sue and Pete McCall, kindly contributed their time and thoughts as they also read my emerging manuscript.

My thanks, also, to Hal Jones, a former CBC colleague and friend of Len Port, for opening the door to Doubleday Canada. I am grateful to everyone at Doubleday who has touched this project, with a special mention of Senior Editor Tim Rostron. My good fortune in my collaboration with an editor continued with Tim. From our very first conversation I knew I was in good hands. Many thanks also to freelance copy editor Beverley Sotolov.

My friends and colleagues at CBC Edmonton in the 1980s gave me a warm and satisfying work environment that helped me get my feet under me, even though most of them did not know at the time what a shattered person they had in their midst.

And there are, as is true for us all, legions of persons known and unknown who have guided, inspired and coloured my thinking, helping me accept myself for stumbling and falling.

As spiritual teacher Ram Dass said, "We're all just walking each other home."